SCALPED

BOOK TWO

JASON AARON
Writer

R. M. GUÉRA
DAVIDE FURNÒ (ISSUES #18-20)
JOHN PAUL LEON (ISSUE #12)
Artists

GIULIA BRUSCO
Colorist

STEVE WANDS
Letterer

R.M GUÉRA
Cover Art

Original series covers by
JOCK
DAVE JOHNSON
TIM BRADSTREET

Introduction by **ED BRUBAKER**

SCALPED created by
JASON AARON and **R. M. GUÉRA**

SCALPED

BOOK TWO

WILL DENNIS Editor - Original Series
CASEY SEIJAS MARK DOYLE Assistant Editors - Original Series
JAMIE S. RICH Group Editor - Vertigo Comics
JEB WOODARD Group Editor - Collected Editions
SCOTT NYBAKKEN Editor - Collected Edition
STEVE COOK Design Dtirector - Books
DAMIAN RYLAND Publication Design

BOB HARRAS Senior VP - Editor-in-Chief, DC Comics
MARK DOYLE Executive Editor, Vertigo

DIANE NELSON President
DAN DiDIO Publisher
JIM LEE Publisher
GEOFF JOHNS President & Chief Creative Officer
AMIT DESAI Executive VP - Business & Marketing Strategy, Direct to Consumer & Global Franchise Management
SAM ADES Senior VP - Direct to Consumer
BOBBIE CHASE VP - Talent Development
MARK CHIARELLO Senior VP - Art, Design & Collected Editions
JOHN CUNNINGHAM Senior VP - Sales & Trade Marketing
ANNE DePIES Senior VP - Business Strategy, Finance & Administration
DON FALLETTI VP - Manufacturing Operations
LAWRENCE GANEM VP - Editorial Administration & Talent Relations
ALISON GILL Senior VP - Manufacturing & Operations
HANK KANALZ Senior VP - Editorial Strategy & Administration
JAY KOGAN VP - Legal Affairs
JACK MAHAN VP - Business Affairs
NICK J. NAPOLITANO VP - Manufacturing Administration
EDDIE SCANNELL VP - Consumer Marketing
COURTNEY SIMMONS Senior VP - Publicity & Communications
JIM (SKI) SOKOLOWSKI VP - Comic Book Specialty Sales & Trade Marketing
NANCY SPEARS VP - Mass, Book, Digital Sales & Trade Marketing
MICHELE R. WELLS VP - Content Strategy

Logo design by JOCK

SCALPED BOOK TWO

DC Comics 2900 West Alameda Ave., Burbank, CA 91505
Printed by LSC Communications, Owensville, MO, USA. 2/9/18.
First Printing. ISBN: 978-1-4012-7786-4

Library of Congress Cataloging-in-Publication Data is available.

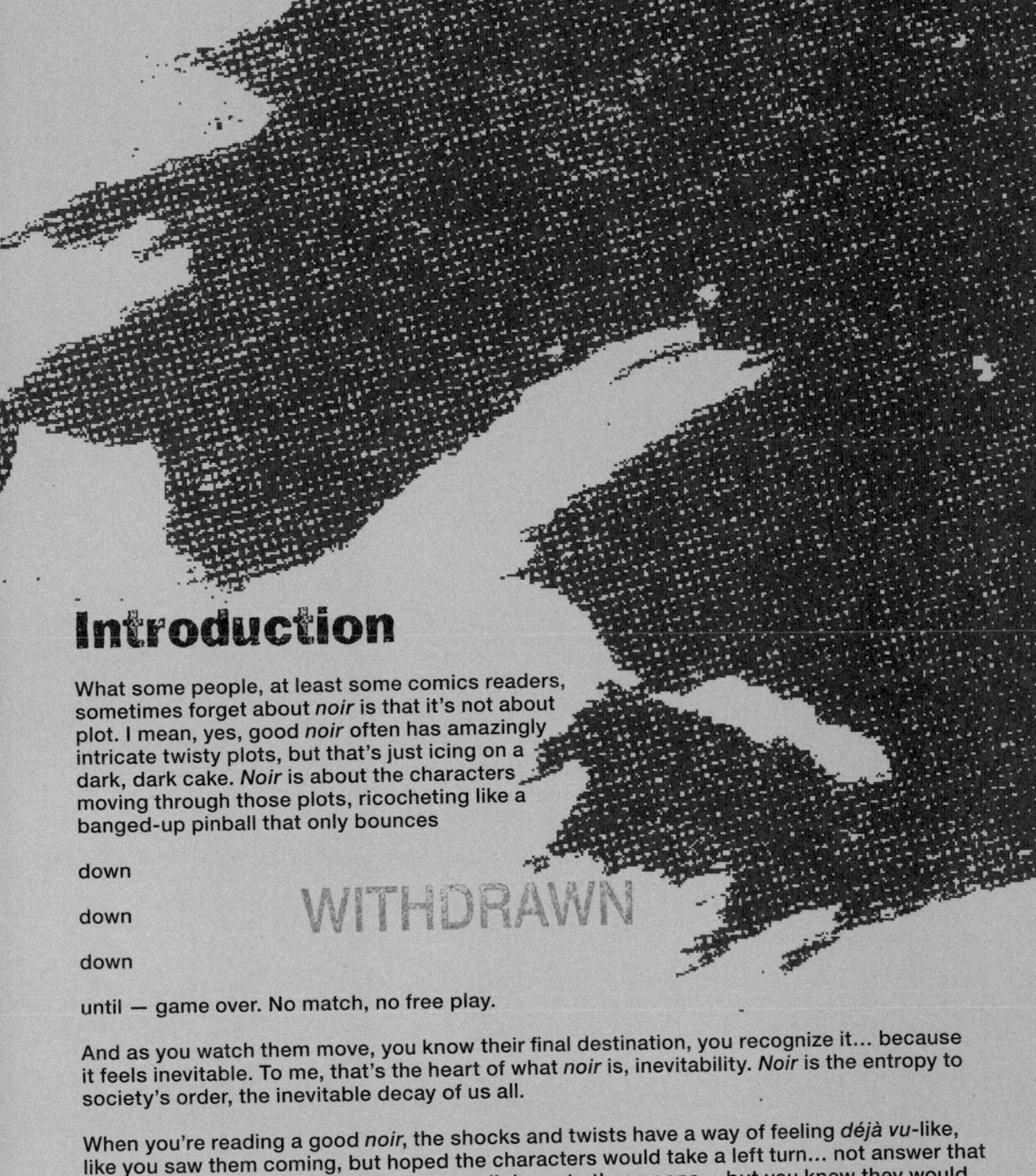

Introduction

What some people, at least some comics readers, sometimes forget about *noir* is that it's not about plot. I mean, yes, good *noir* often has amazingly intricate twisty plots, but that's just icing on a dark, dark cake. *Noir* is about the characters moving through those plots, ricocheting like a banged-up pinball that only bounces

down

down

down

WITHDRAWN

until — game over. No match, no free play.

And as you watch them move, you know their final destination, you recognize it... because it feels inevitable. To me, that's the heart of what *noir* is, inevitability. *Noir* is the entropy to society's order, the inevitable decay of us all.

When you're reading a good *noir*, the shocks and twists have a way of feeling *déjà vu*-like, like you saw them coming, but hoped the characters would take a left turn... not answer that phone, not sleep with that woman, not sell drugs to those cops... but you knew they would. It would have been wrong if they didn't, and the real surprise can be that you care about someone you know is in for hell. You relate to them, even when their hell is so much bigger than your own. But we're all going to die, and we all make mistakes.

The best *noir* stories make you forget plot entirely by giving you characters that feel so well-realized you can't look away as they

fall

fall

fall

and set-ups that feel so real that you want to run from them screaming.

That's what SCALPED is like.

For three years in the early part of this decade, my wife and I lived on a farm in Mendocino County in a valley that had once been entirely Indian land. About half of the valley was still a reservation, and the town was split up among Indians and cowboys — it had its fair share of farmers and ranchers and hippies and pot growers, but it really came down to cowboys and

Indians at the end of the day. So I know a bit about Indian life in modern America.

I've done ride-alongs in sheriff's cars and listened to stories of abuse and self-hatred and fear. And I've seen their celebrations and listened to stories of proud history and magic.

And it feels like Jason Aaron has, too. I know he's making this all up, but his depiction of this once-proud people staggering toward their inevitable demise feels very real to me. And I think the guys on the rez, from the drunks and speed-freaks at the car graveyards, to the activists on the Tribal Council, would recognize that, too.

The valley I lived in was referred to by the sheriff's department as "a target-rich environment." A lot of desperate people, a lot of drugs and alcohol, a lot of guns, all in close proximity. That is the world of SCALPED. It's a target-rich environment, and no book proves it more than this one.

Tapping into the heart of *noir*, Jason Aaron tells a story that is really many stories, and which all have the same ending. It doesn't get much more inevitable (there's that word again) than knowing the ending through most of the book — but here's the key... you don't care. You turn each page just as fast, maybe faster, wanting to know how each character winds their way toward that conclusion.

And that's why I love *noir*, and why SCALPED is a work of art.

Ed Brubaker
January 2009

Award-winning writer Ed Brubaker is the co-creator of CRIMINAL, INCOGNITO, SLEEPER and GOTHAM CENTRAL, among others. He has also written BATMAN, CATWOMAN, Captain America and Daredevil. He lives in Seattle, Washington, with his wife, Melanie, and many pets.

DREAMING HIMSELF INTO THE REAL WORLD

SOMETIMES IT'S A KNIFE.

OTHER TIMES A GUN.

BUT EITHER WAY, THE RESULT IS ALWAYS THE SAME.

I LOSE. I FAIL. I FUCK UP.

I DIE.

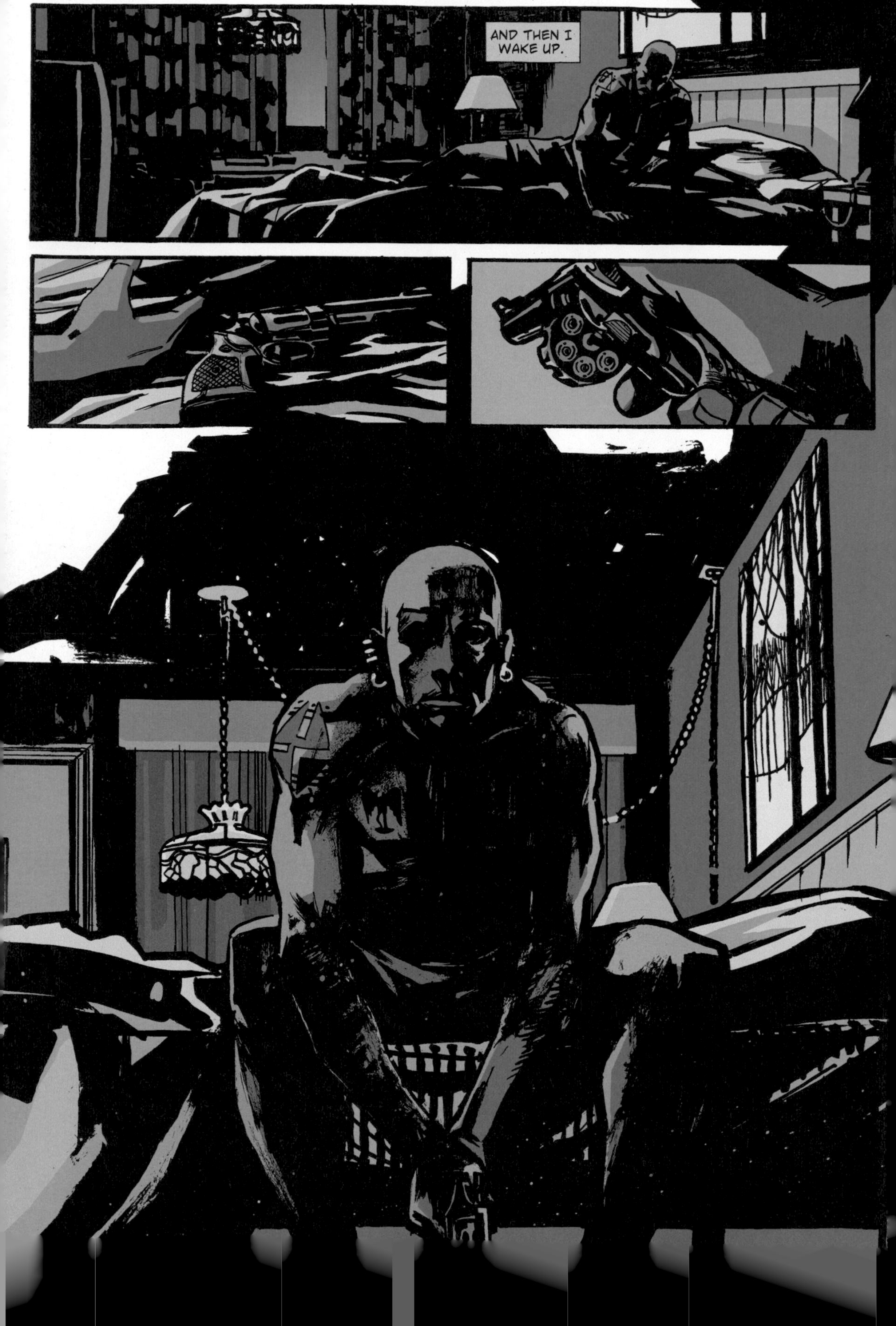
AND THEN I WAKE UP.

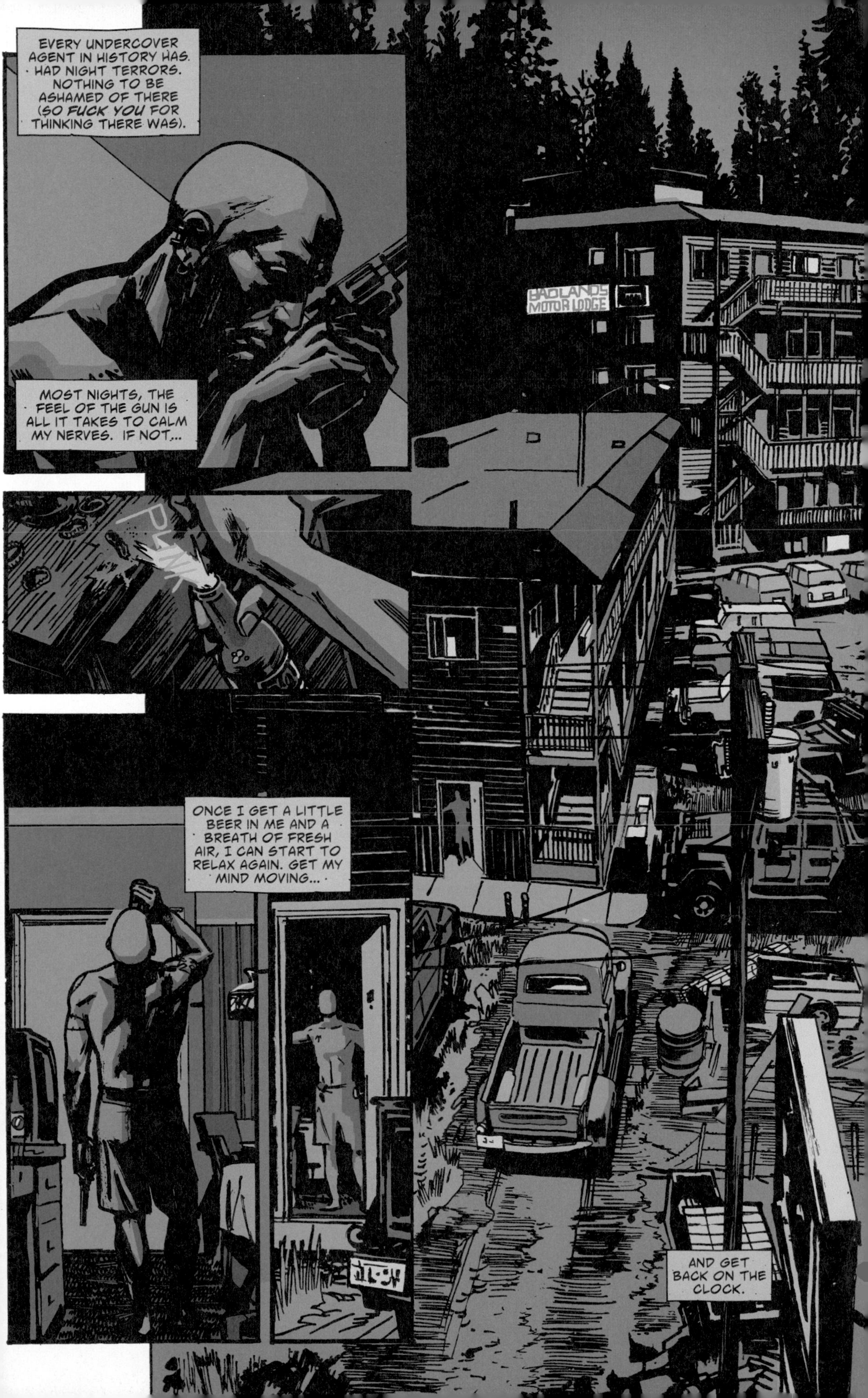
EVERY UNDERCOVER AGENT IN HISTORY HAS HAD NIGHT TERRORS. NOTHING TO BE ASHAMED OF THERE (SO FUCK YOU FOR THINKING THERE WAS).
MOST NIGHTS, THE FEEL OF THE GUN IS ALL IT TAKES TO CALM MY NERVES. IF NOT...
PLINK
ONCE I GET A LITTLE BEER IN ME AND A BREATH OF FRESH AIR, I CAN START TO RELAX AGAIN. GET MY MIND MOVING...
BADLANDS MOTOR LODGE
AND GET BACK ON THE CLOCK.

IT'S ALMOST FOUR IN THE MORNING, SO THERE GOES TOM SLIDELL, ONLY FORTY MINUTES LATE AS HE HEADS OUT TO OVERSEE THE SHIFT CHANGE AT THE HUGE CHICKEN RANCH METH HOUSE ON ROUTE 18.

AS *DUMB* AS *THAT* MOTHERFUCKER IS, IT'S A WONDER THAT PLACE AIN'T EXPLODED YET.

A FEW DOORS DOWN, I CAN MAKE OUT THE MOANS OF SOME OF THE WHORES FROM THE POWWOW WOW STRIP CLUB.

NO DOUBT WORKING OFF A FEW *IRREGULARITIES* IN THE NIGHT'S BOOKKEEPING.

A FEW DOORS DOWN FROM THAT, I KNOW BIG TIM TWO BONES HAS A SUITCASE UNDER HIS BED FILLED WITH 40 KEYS OF UNCUT COKE HE BOUGHT OFF A WYOMING STATE TROOPER.

BILLY RED BEAR IN 5A HAS A BATHTUB FILLED WITH AK-47S.

THE BOYS IN ROOM 18 KEEP AN ICE BUCKET FULL OF *EARS*.

WELCOME TO THE BADLANDS MOTOR LODGE, THE BUNKHOUSE FOR RED CROW'S DAWG SOLDIERZ. GROUND ZERO FOR HIS CRIMINAL EMPIRE (IF YOU WANNA FUCKIN' CALL IT THAT).

I COULD MAKE CASES ON EVERY MOTHERFUCKER IN HERE WITH WHAT I HAVE RIGHT NOW, BUT GUESS WHAT?

I AIN'T GONNA DO THAT. *EVER.*

'CAUSE THAT *AIN'T* WHY I'M HERE.

THAT NITZ BASTARD... HE'S GONNA GET YOU *KILLED.*

LISTEN TO YOUR OLD "UNCLE" RED CROW, KID. I MAY HAVE *FUCKED* YOUR MOTHER, BUT THAT DON'T MAKE ME YOUR *DADDY.*

IF I FIGURE OUT YOU'RE WORKING WITH THE FEDS, I WILL NOT HESITATE TO *KILL* YOU.

I WILL DO IT MY *OWN* DAMN SELF IF I HAVE TO. TRUST ME, I'VE KILLED PEOPLE YOUNGER AND SMARTER THAN YOU.

I'M *SUSPICIOUS* OF YA ALREADY, YA KNOW THAT? HOW MUCH LONGER BEFORE YOU SLIP UP AND I GET WISE?

YA ASK ME, THE SMART MONEY'S ON...

"ANY *FUCKING* DAY NOW."

RULE NUMBER ONE OF THE UNDERCOVER AGENT: *NEVER* GET INVOLVED IN IMPROPER SEXUAL RELATIONSHIPS.

WHOOPS, GUESS YOU FUCKED THAT ONE UP ALREADY, HUH, HOSS?

THE *TRASHIER* I AM, THE MORE YOU WANT ME, AM I RIGHT? WHAT SORT OF *DEEP-SEEDED* PSYCHOSIS IS THAT, I WONDER?

THOUGH A BETTER QUESTION IS...

HOW MUCH *LOWER* WILL YOU GO, JUST TO GET YOUR ROCKS OFF?

PERSONALLY, I'M *WET* WITH ANTICIPATION.

WHADDA YA SAY TO *THAT*, LOVER?

FLUUUSSH

DAMN. WEIRD-ASS DREAM.

THAT'S THE LAST TIME I EAT BARBECUE AT 2 AM.

KRRCH. DISPATCH, THIS IS CAR 12, RESPONDING TO A 911, COME IN...

TIME NOW TO BRUSH ASIDE THE CRAZY DREAMS.

AND FOCUS.

WITHOUT FOCUS, I'M DEAD.

I CAME HERE TO DO A JOB, AND THAT'S WHAT THE HELL I'M DOING.

I AIN'T LOOKING TO MAKE UP WITH DEAR OLD MOMMY OR GET IN TOUCH WITH MY INJUN ROOTS.

AIN'T LOOKING FOR TRUE LOVE OR GOD OR ANY OTHER SUCH MAKE-BELIEVE BULLSHIT.

YOU CAN BET YOUR ASS, AIN'T NOTHING IN THE WORLD CAN HOLD ME HERE ONCE THIS GODDAMN JOB IS DONE.

AND IT'LL BE DONE MOST DIRECTLY, I ASSURE YOU.

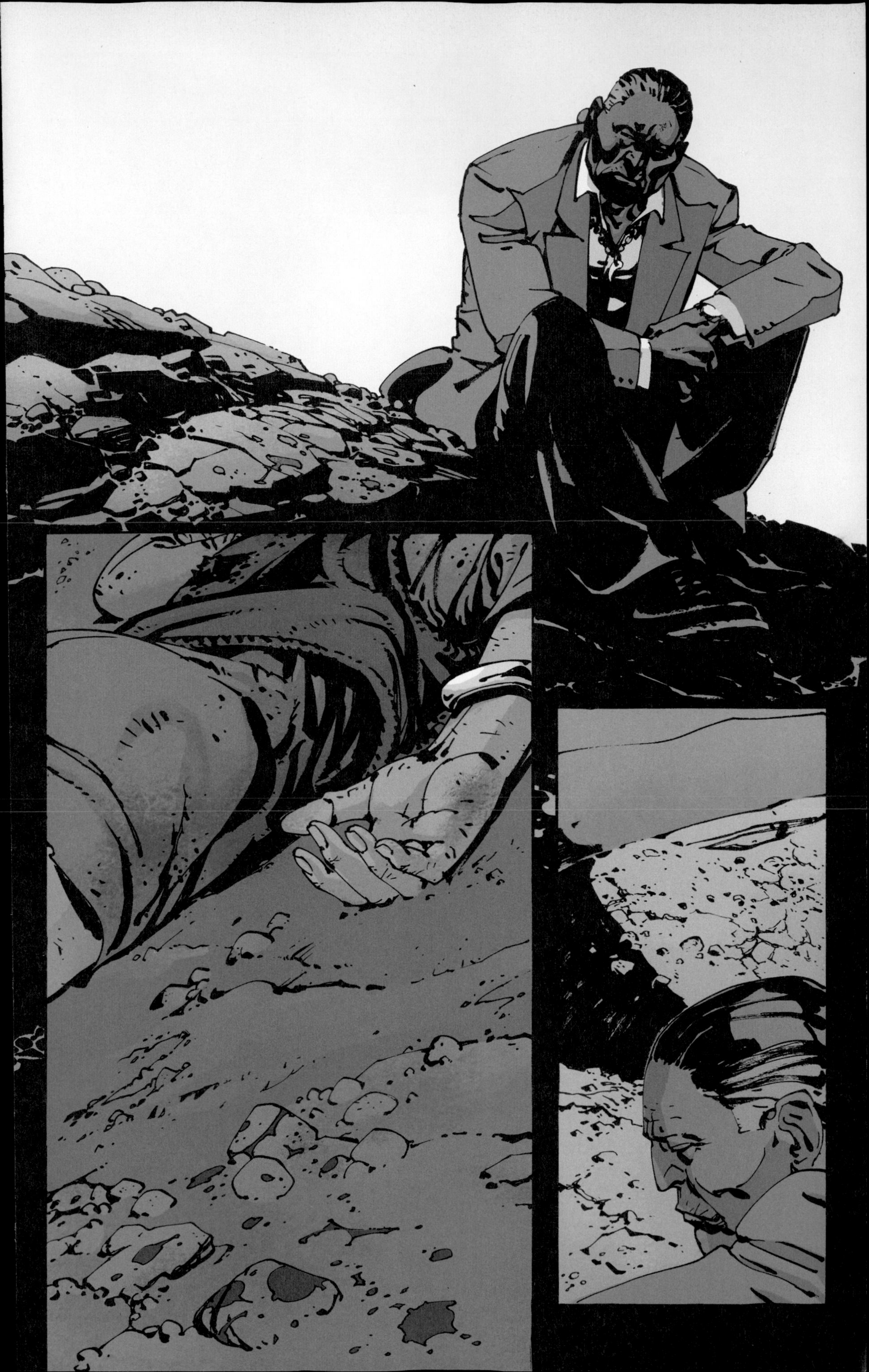

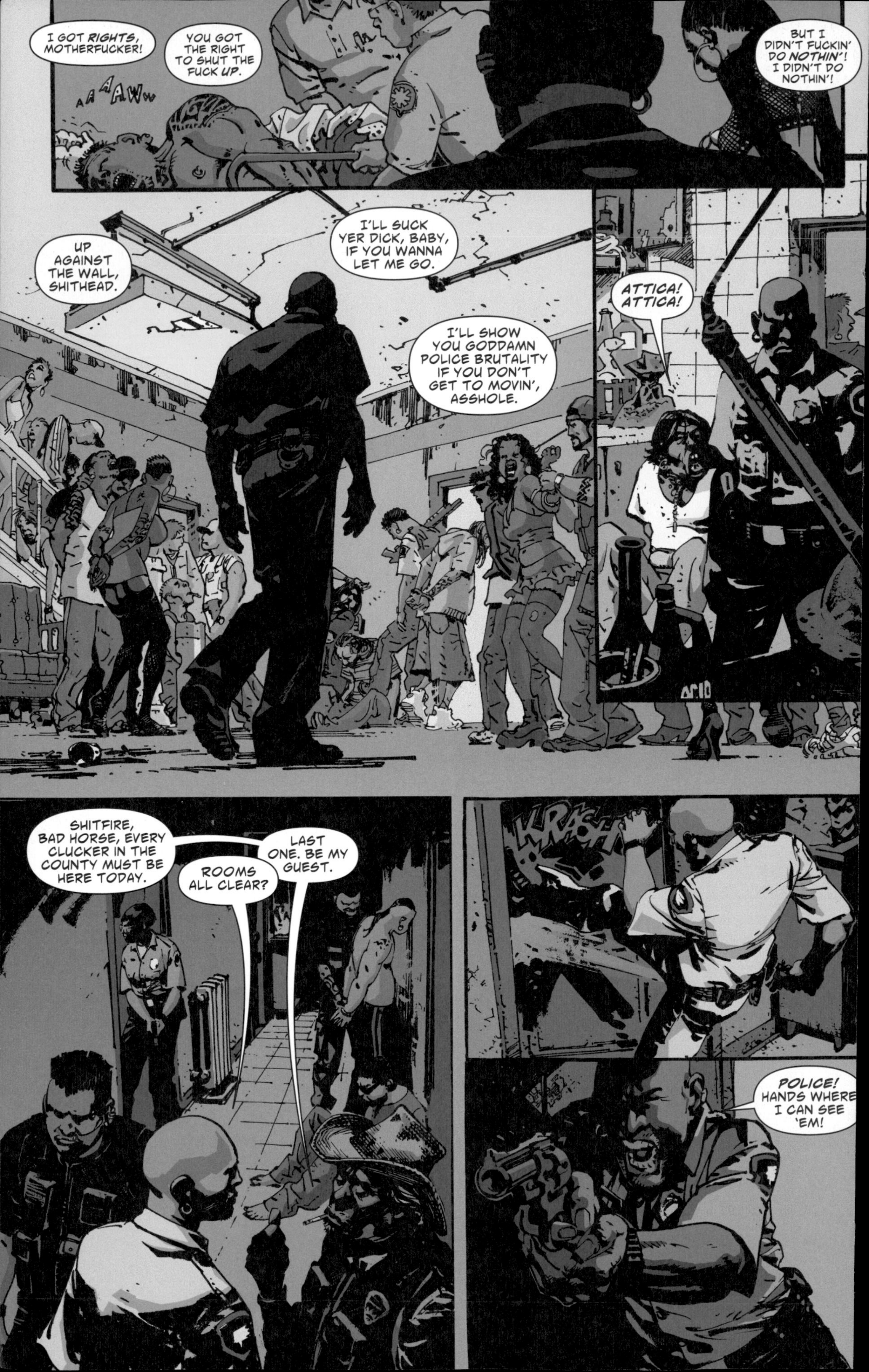
I GOT RIGHTS, MOTHERFUCKER!
YOU GOT THE RIGHT TO SHUT THE FUCK UP.
AAAAWW
BUT I DIDN'T FUCKIN' DO NOTHIN'! I DIDN'T DO NOTHIN'!
UP AGAINST THE WALL, SHITHEAD.
I'LL SUCK YER DICK, BABY, IF YOU WANNA LET ME GO.
I'LL SHOW YOU GODDAMN POLICE BRUTALITY IF YOU DON'T GET TO MOVIN', ASSHOLE.
ATTICA! ATTICA!
SHITFIRE, BAD HORSE, EVERY CLUCKER IN THE COUNTY MUST BE HERE TODAY.
ROOMS ALL CLEAR?
LAST ONE. BE MY GUEST.
KRASH
POLICE! HANDS WHERE I CAN SEE 'EM!

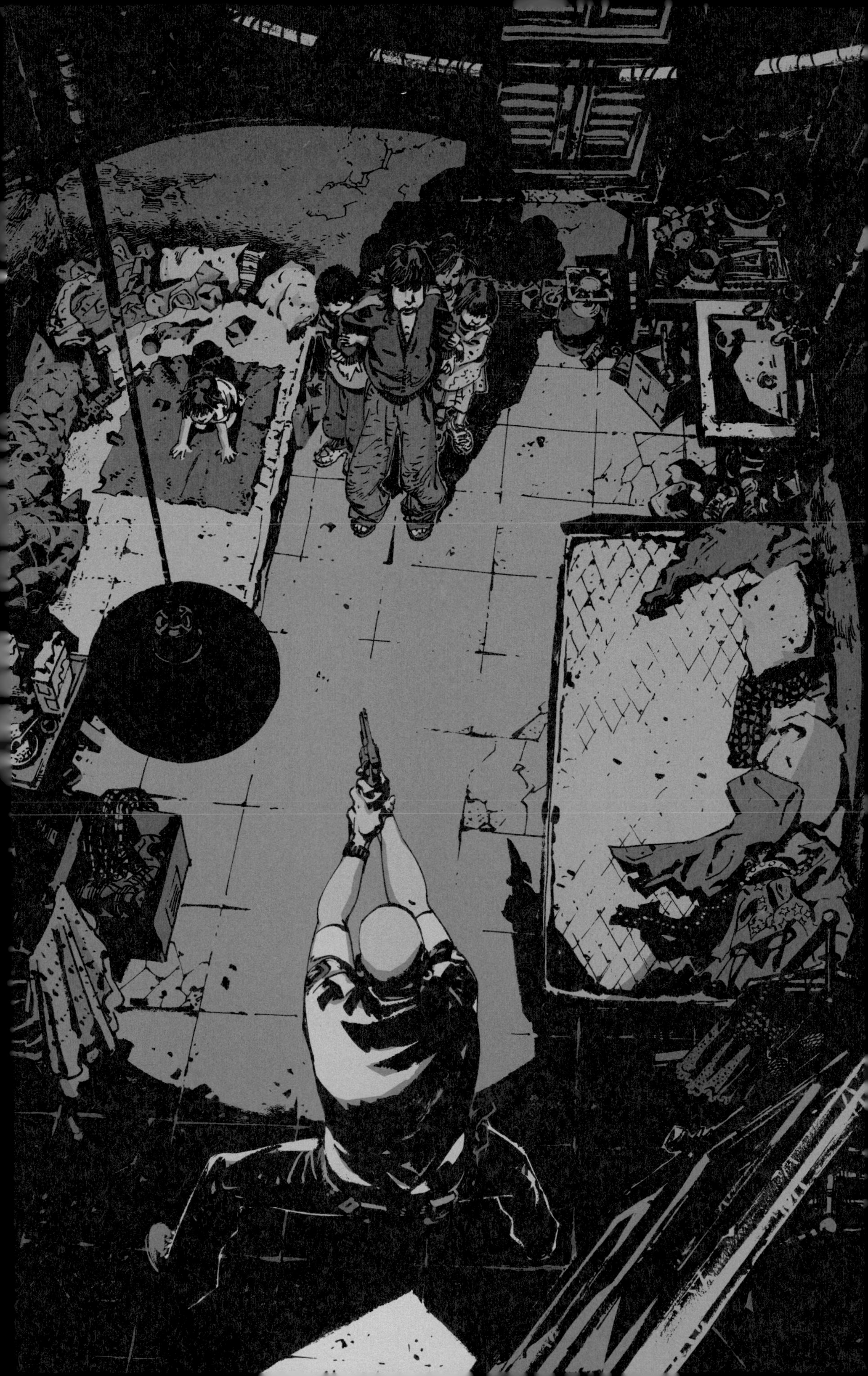

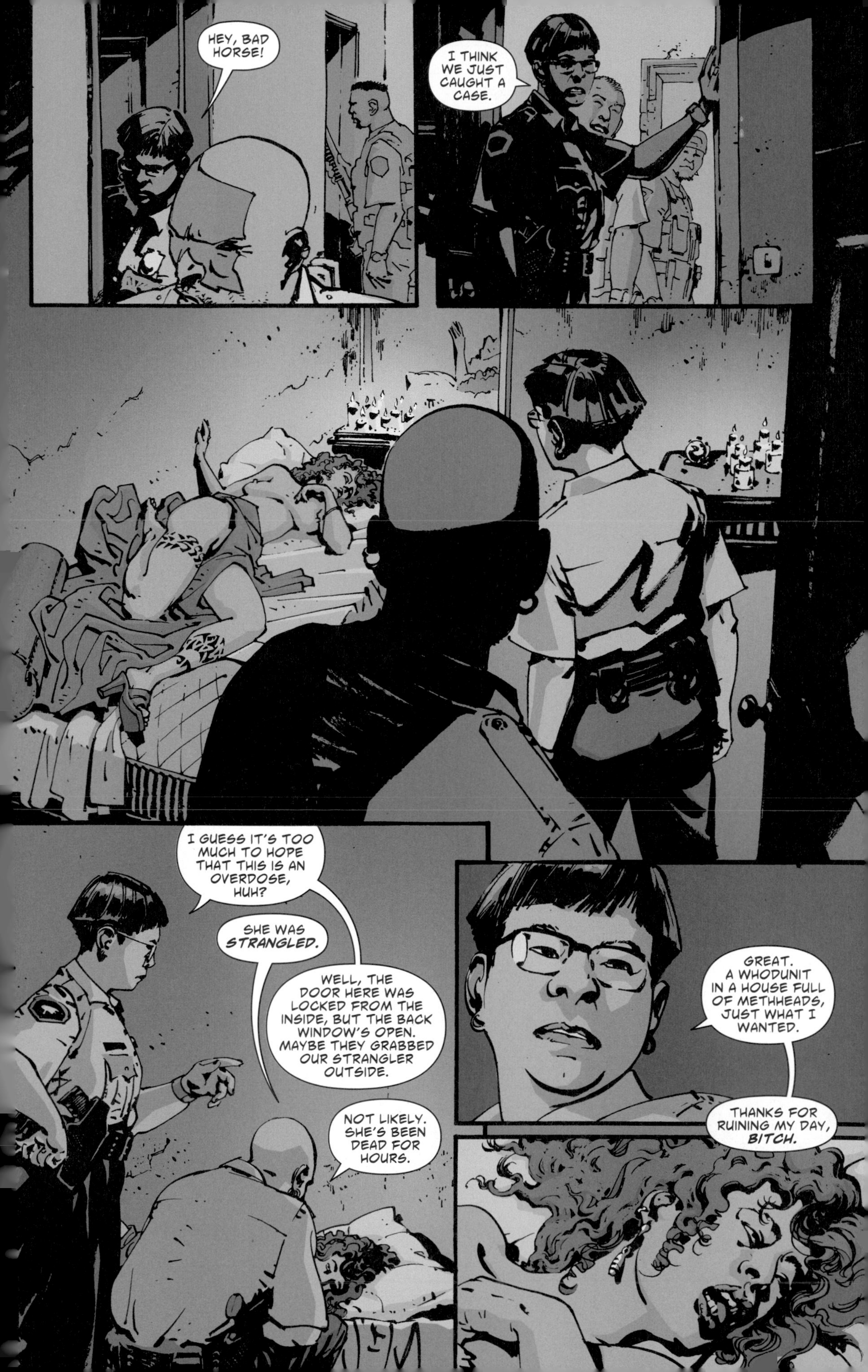
HEY, BAD HORSE!
I THINK WE JUST CAUGHT A CASE.
I GUESS IT'S TOO MUCH TO HOPE THAT THIS IS AN OVERDOSE, HUH?
SHE WAS *STRANGLED.*
WELL, THE DOOR HERE WAS LOCKED FROM THE INSIDE, BUT THE BACK WINDOW'S OPEN. MAYBE THEY GRABBED OUR STRANGLER OUTSIDE.
NOT LIKELY. SHE'S BEEN DEAD FOR HOURS.
GREAT. A WHODUNIT IN A HOUSE FULL OF METHHEADS, JUST WHAT I WANTED.
THANKS FOR RUINING MY DAY, *BITCH.*

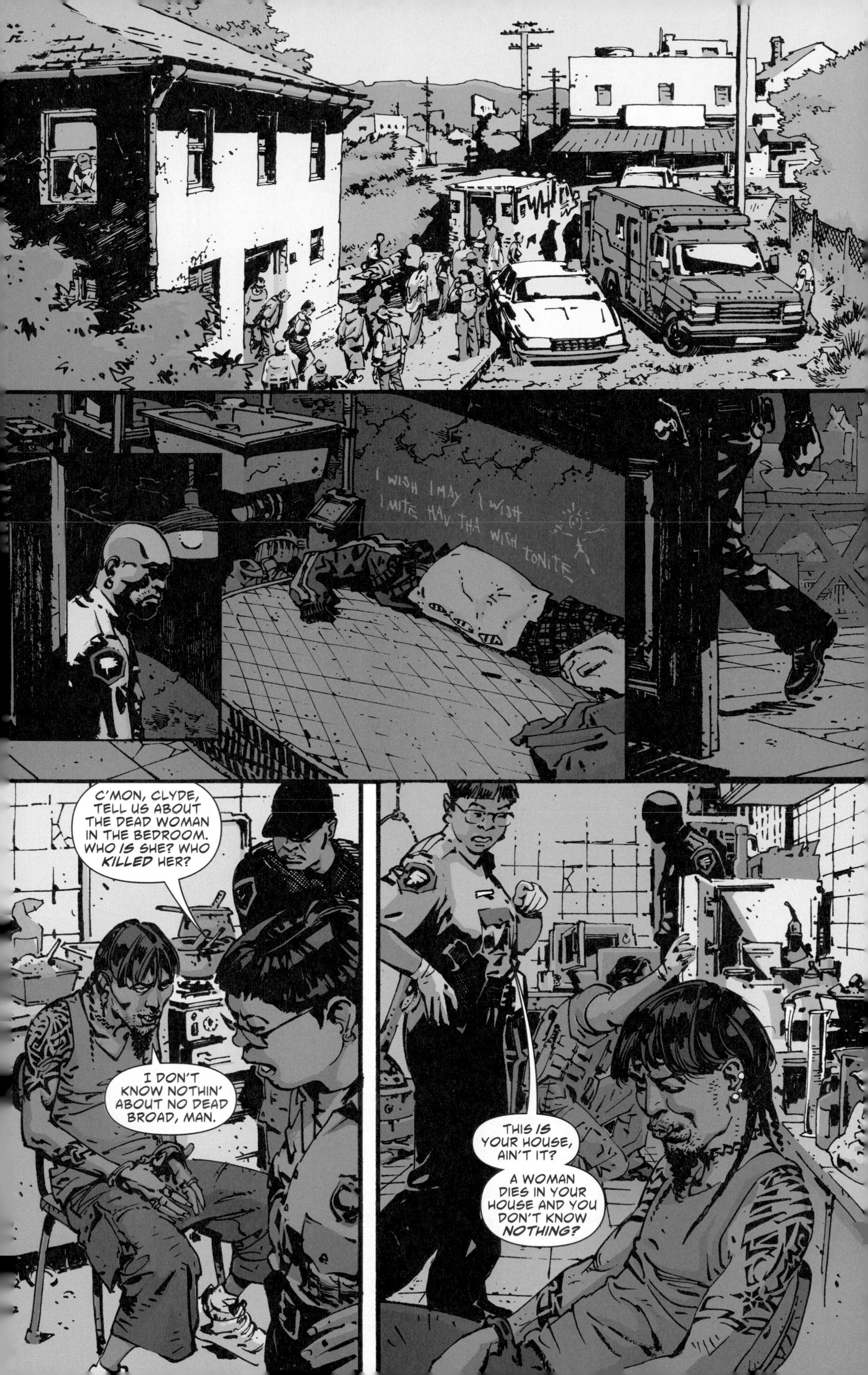
I WISH I MAY I WISH
I MITE HAV THA WISH TONITE
C'MON, CLYDE, TELL US ABOUT THE DEAD WOMAN IN THE BEDROOM. WHO *IS* SHE? WHO *KILLED* HER?
I DON'T KNOW NOTHIN' ABOUT NO DEAD BROAD, MAN.
THIS *IS* YOUR HOUSE, AIN'T IT?
A WOMAN DIES IN YOUR HOUSE AND YOU DON'T KNOW *NOTHING?*

"BREAKS YOUR HEART, DON'T IT?"

I TELL YA, SOME PEOPLE OUGHT *NEVER* HAVE KIDS, HUH?

THEY KNOW ABOUT THEIR MOTHER YET?

NAW. AIN'T NONE OF US HAD THE GUTS TO TELL 'EM.

THEY SAY *ANYTHING* AT ALL?

"THE LITTLE ONES ASKED ABOUT HER A FEW TIMES. THE OLDEST ONE, *SHELTON*, HE KNOWS *SOMETHING'S* UP.

"KID'S ONLY *TWELVE*, BUT HE'S OBVIOUSLY USED TO WATCHING OUT FOR THE OTHERS."

I BOUGHT 'EM ALL CHEESEBURGERS. FIRST THING SHELTON DID WAS TAKE HIS AND TEAR IT INTO *FIVE PIECES*, AND GIVE EACH KID A PIECE.

WHEN I SHOWED HIM THAT THEY EACH HAD THEIR *OWN* BURGER, I THOUGHT HE WAS GONNA *CRY*.

I CAN'T EVEN *IMAGINE* THE SHIT THEM KIDS HAVE BEEN THROUGH.

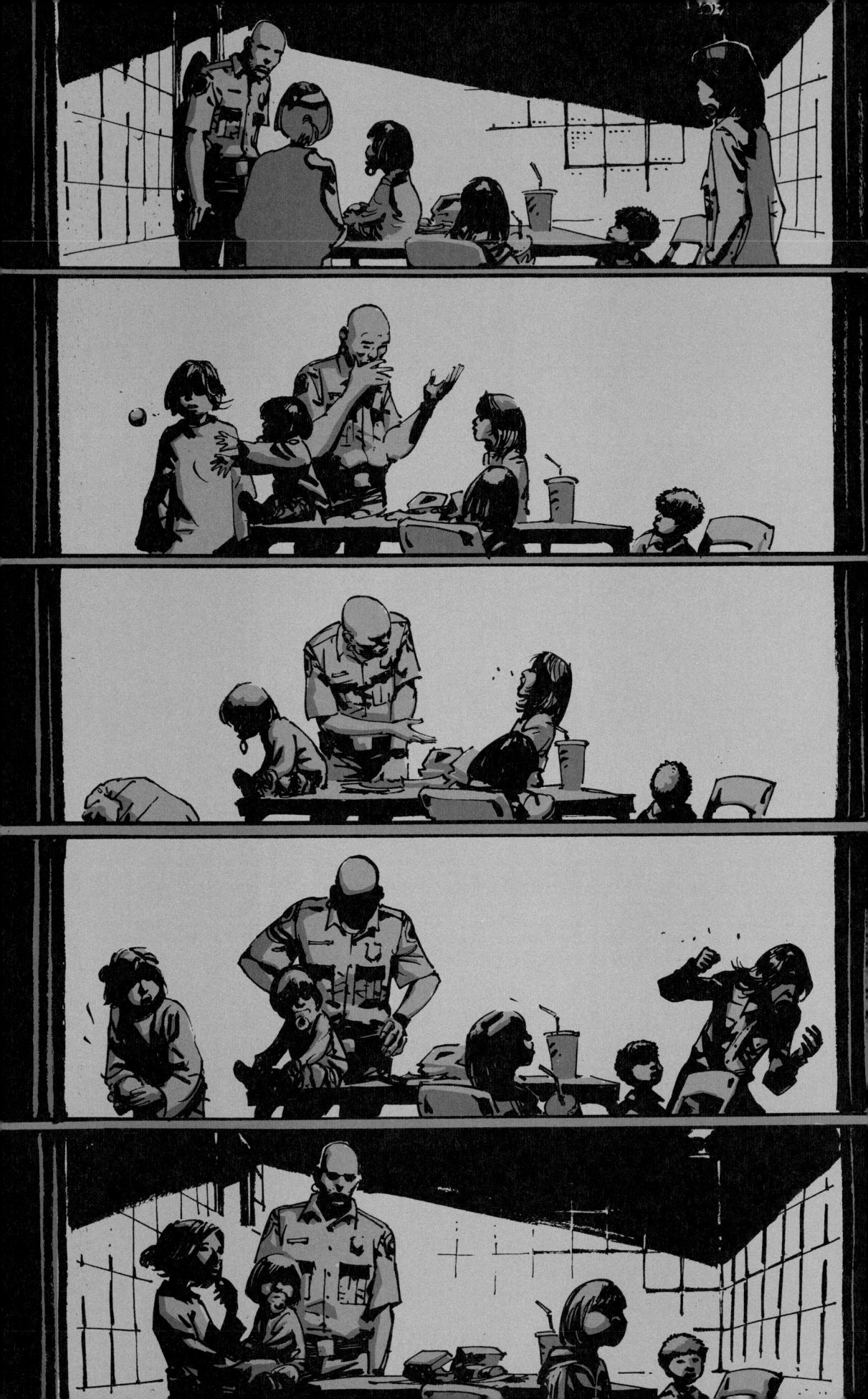

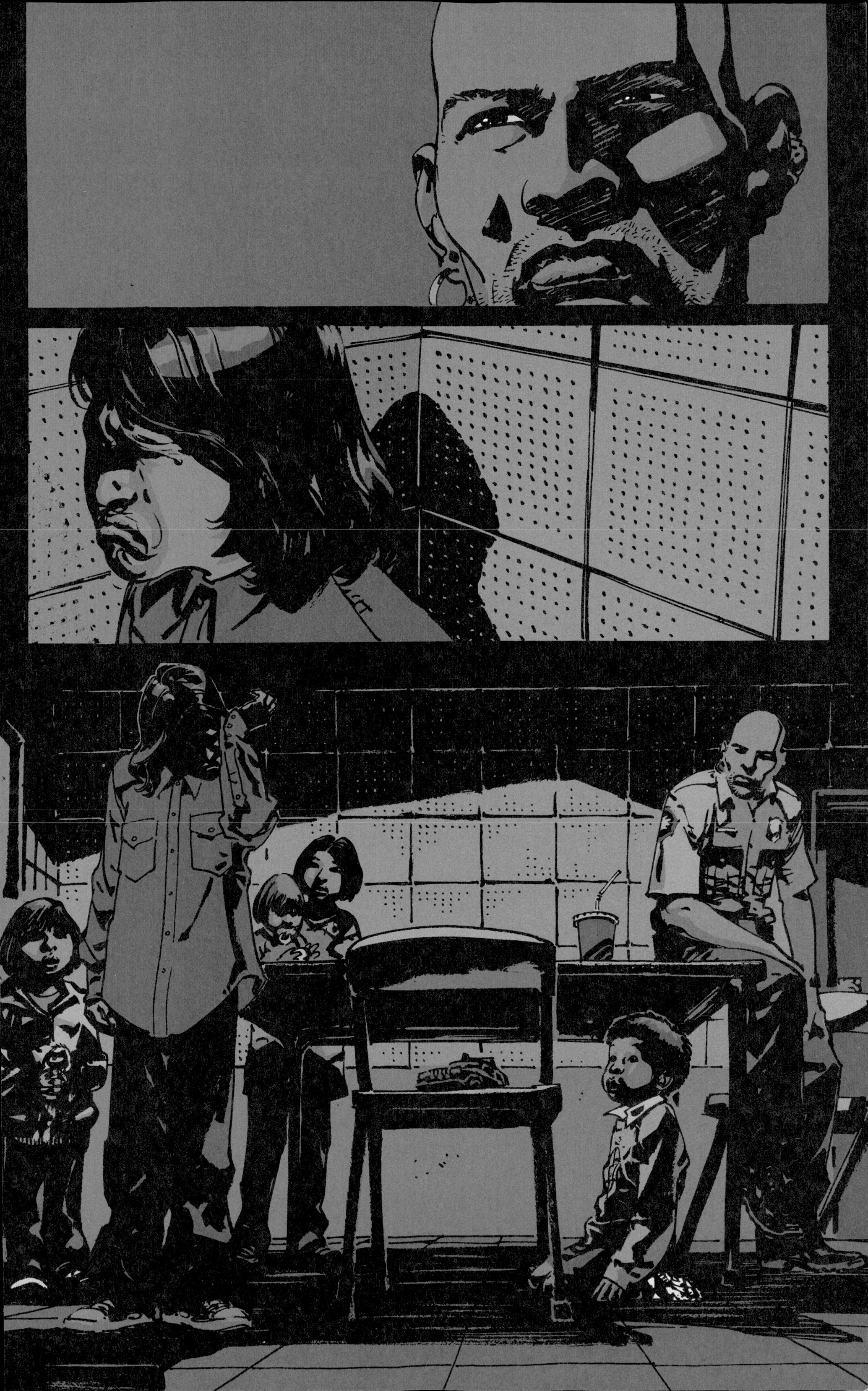

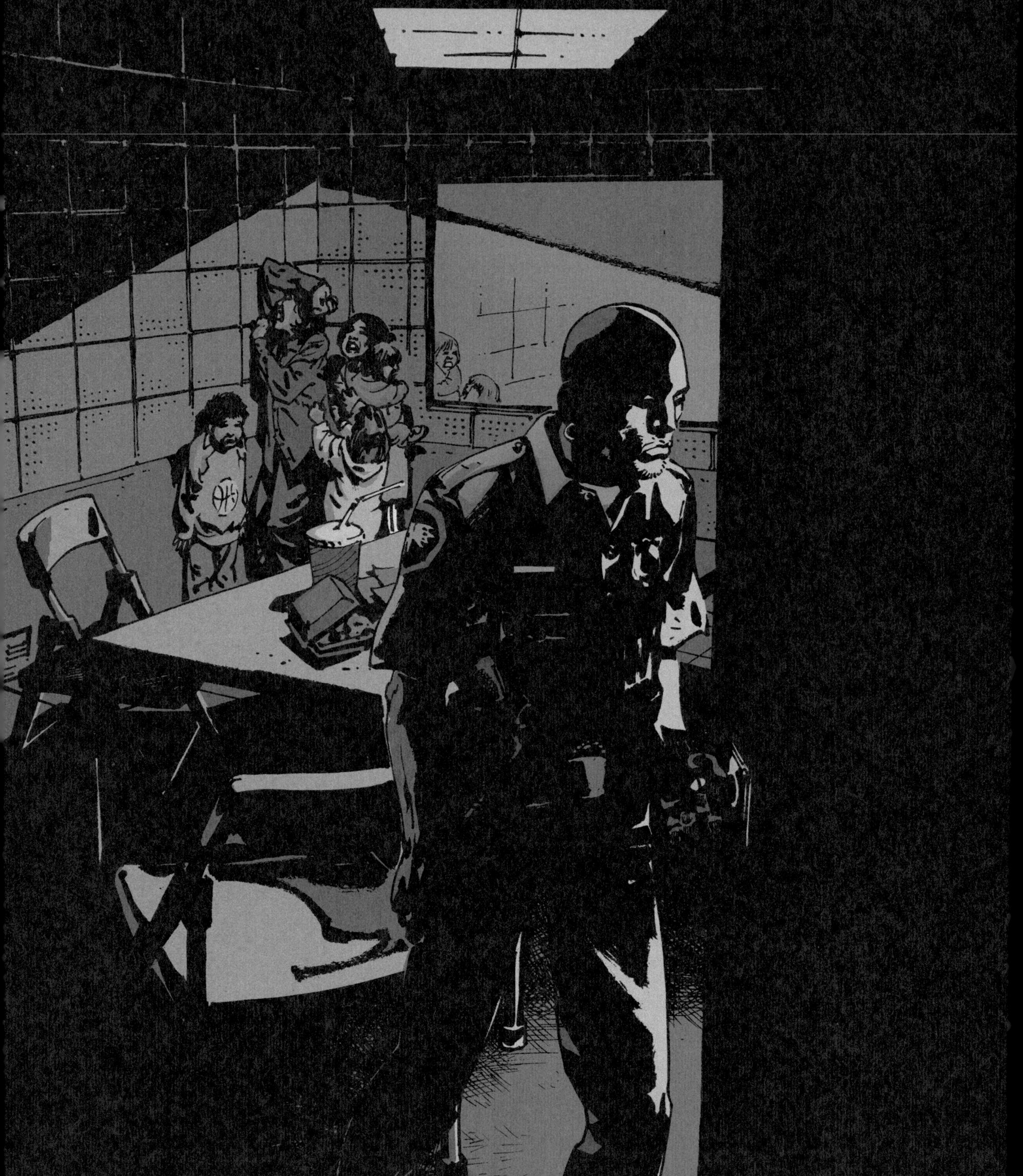

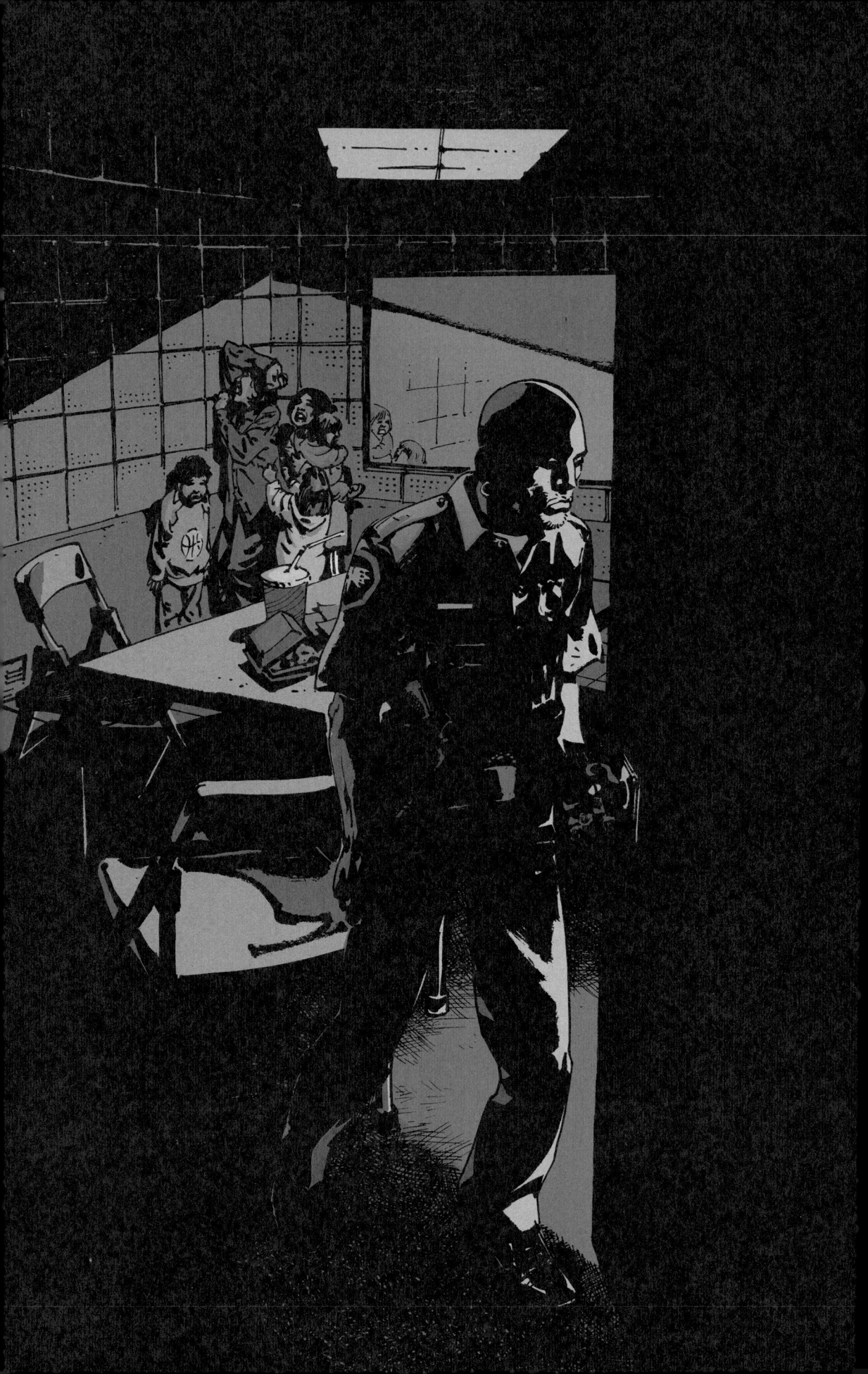

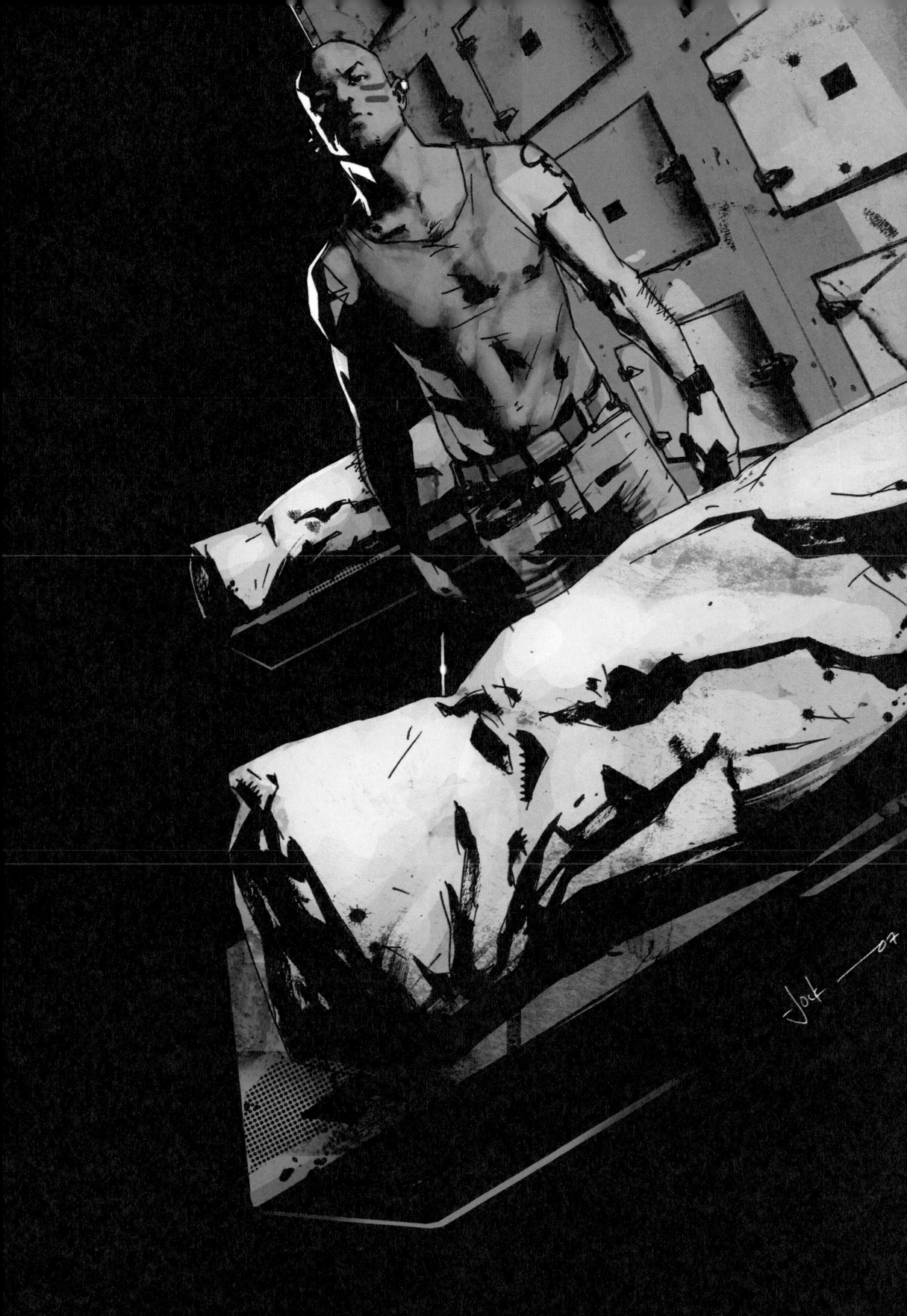

DEAD MOTHERS PART TWO

THE PRESENT.
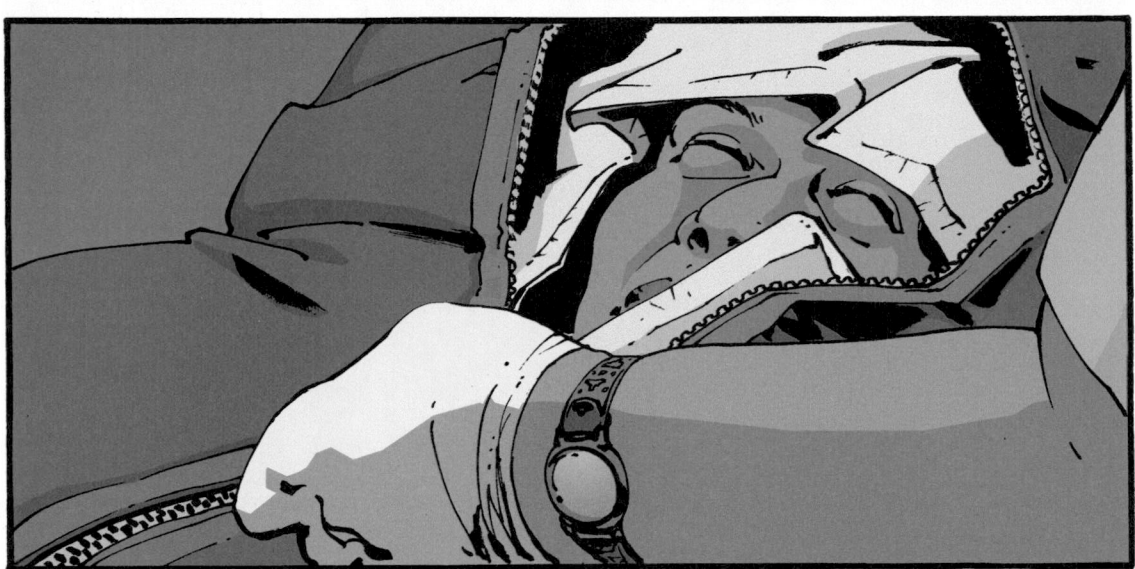

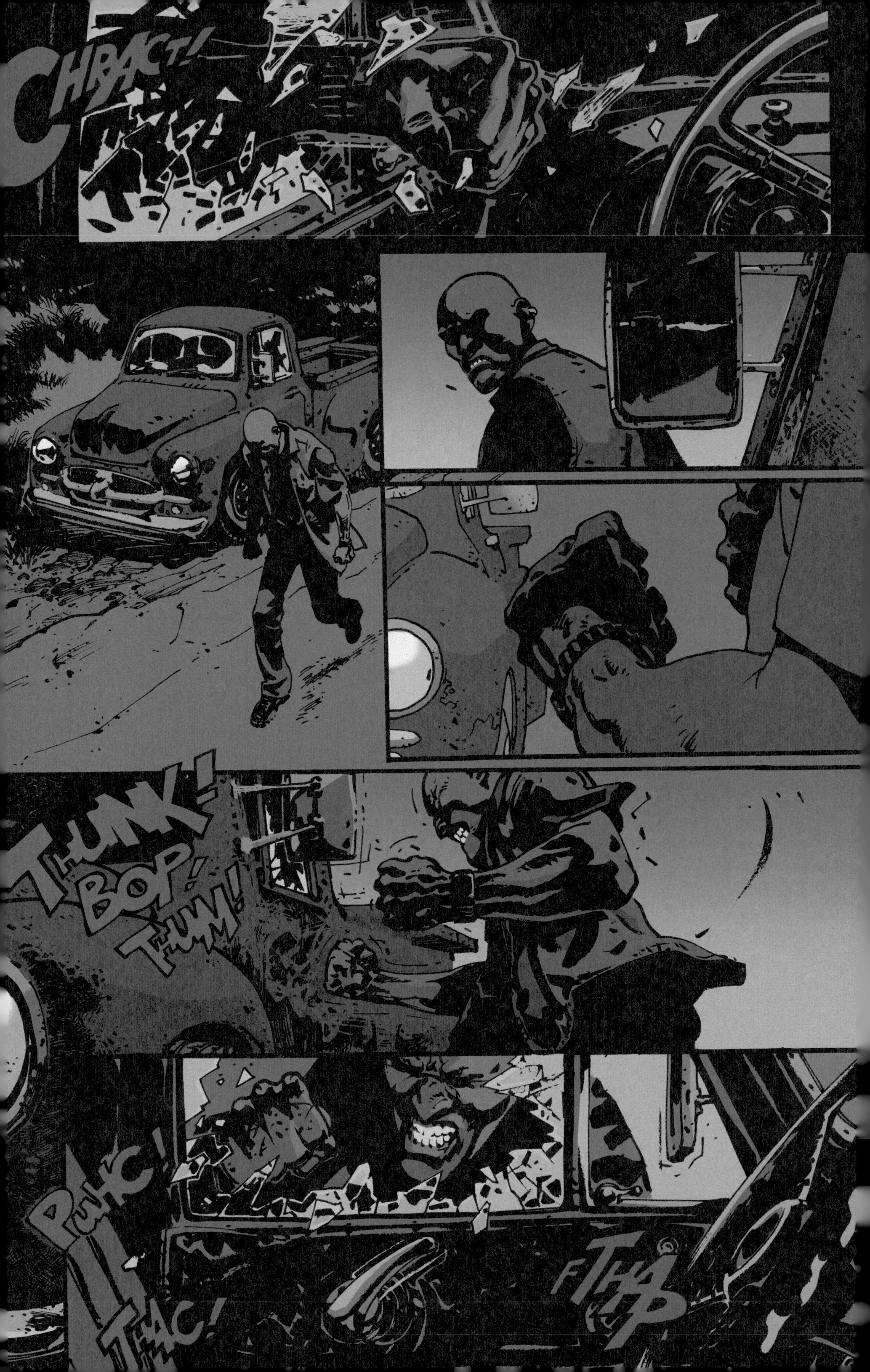
CHRACT!
THUNK!
BOP!
THUM!
PUHC!
THAC!
FTHP

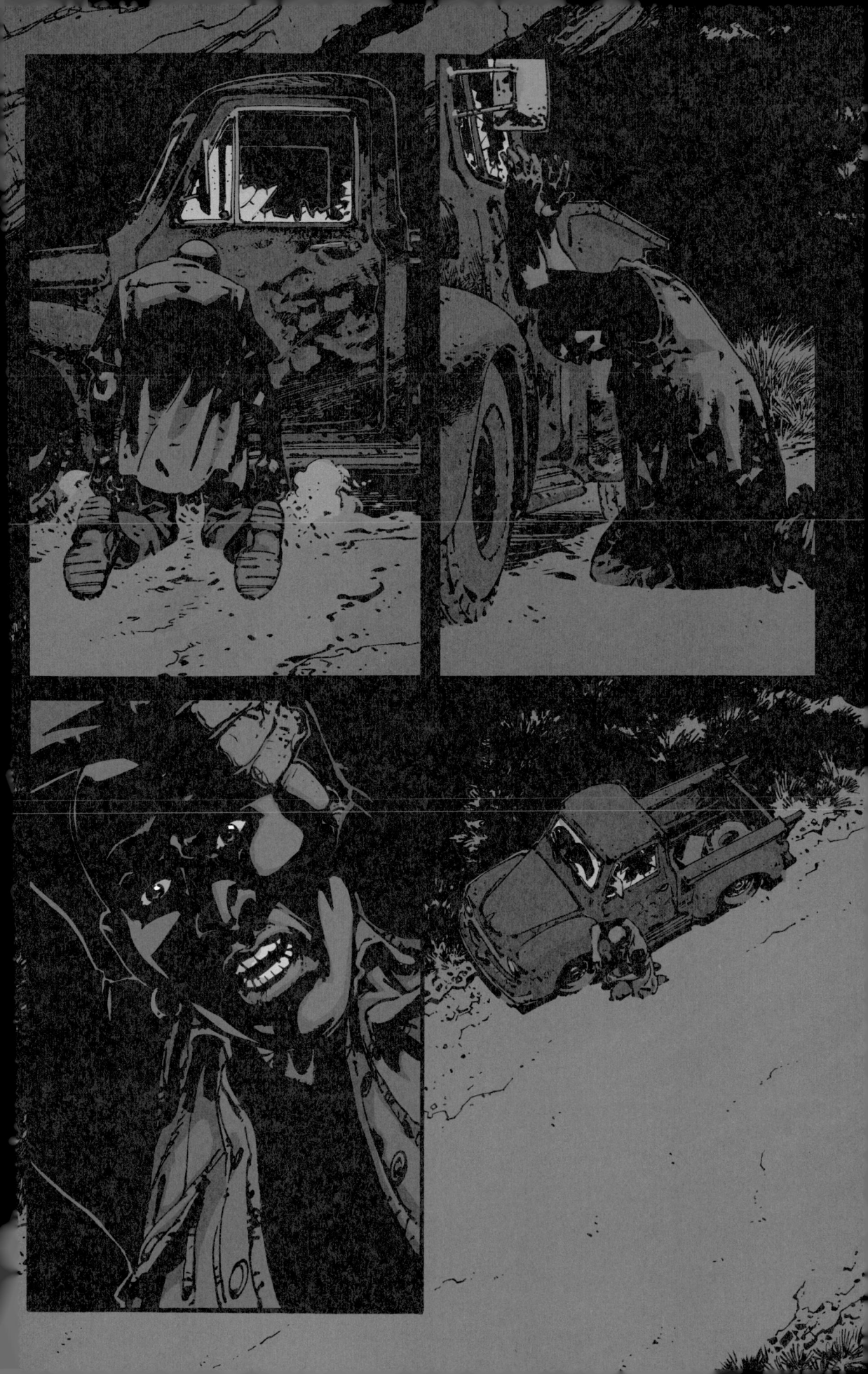

DID YOU FUCKING KILL HER!?

NO, I DIDN'T.

THEN WHO THE FUCK DID?

WE GOT BIGGER PROBLEMS THAN THAT. I WAS TRYING TO TELL YOU...

I'M NOT INTERRUPTING ANYTHING, AM I?

YOU MUST BE CHIEF RED CROW.

I BELIEVE YOU WERE MADE AWARE OF MY IMPENDING VISIT, AM I CORRECT?

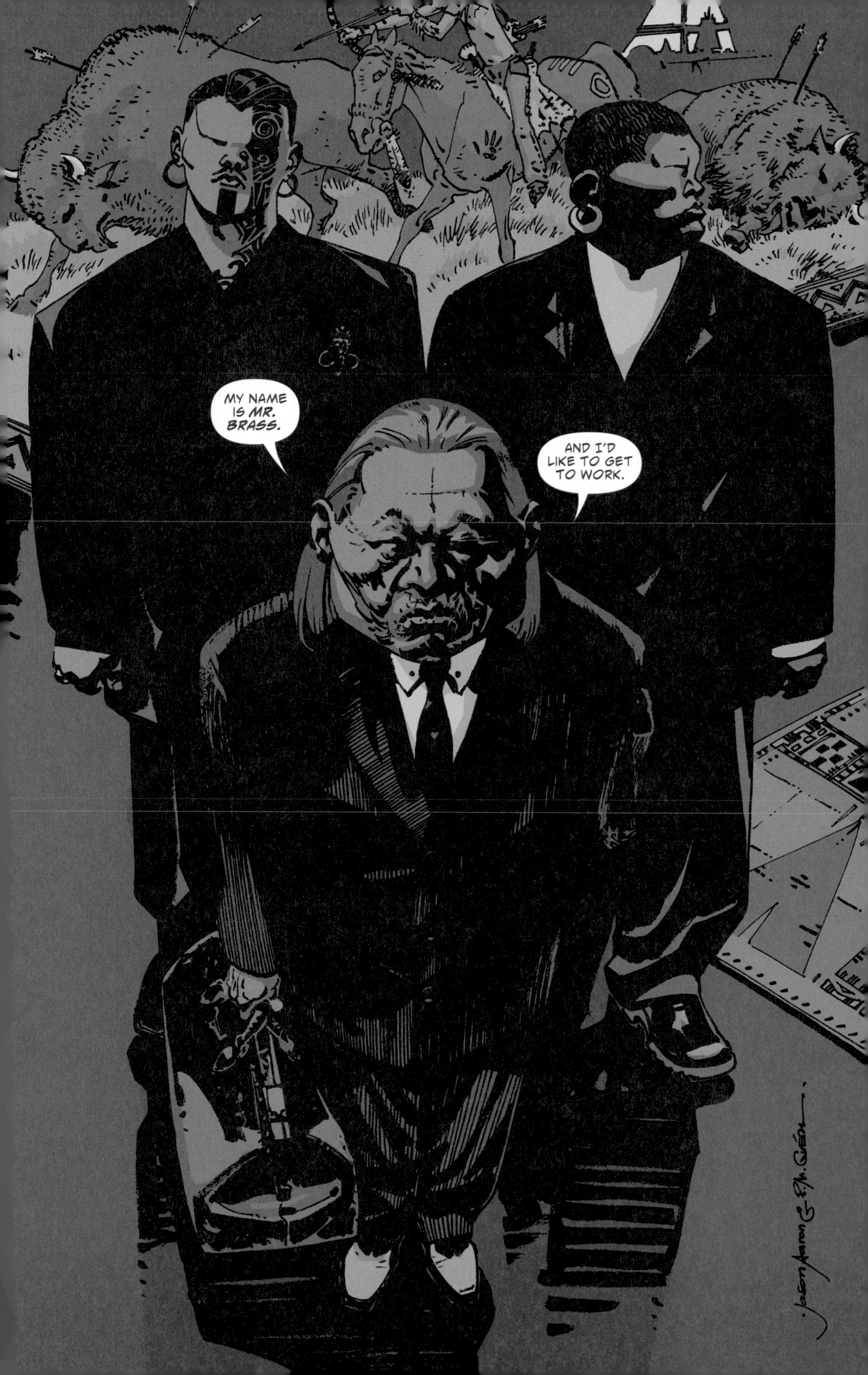
MY NAME IS MR. BRASS.
AND I'D LIKE TO GET TO WORK.

DEAD MOTHERS PART THREE

WHAT WAS ALL THAT ABOUT?
NOTHIN', SHELTON. HAND ME ONE A' THEM BEERS.
YOUR MOM... SHE'S DEAD TOO, RIGHT?
I HEARD SOME PEOPLE TALKING ABOUT IT.
THEY SAID SHE GOT KILLED, SAME AS MY MOM.
YOU GONNA HAND ME ONE A' THEM BEERS OR NOT?
DON'T YOU MISS HER?
ME N' MY MOM... WE JUST DIDN'...
WE WAS JUST NEVER ALL THAT CLOSE.
SHE WAS STILL YOUR MOM THOUGH.
MY MOM WASN'T SO GREAT EITHER. BUT I STILL ALWAYS LOVED HER.
LOOK, KID, YOU WANNA TALK ALL DAMN DAY...

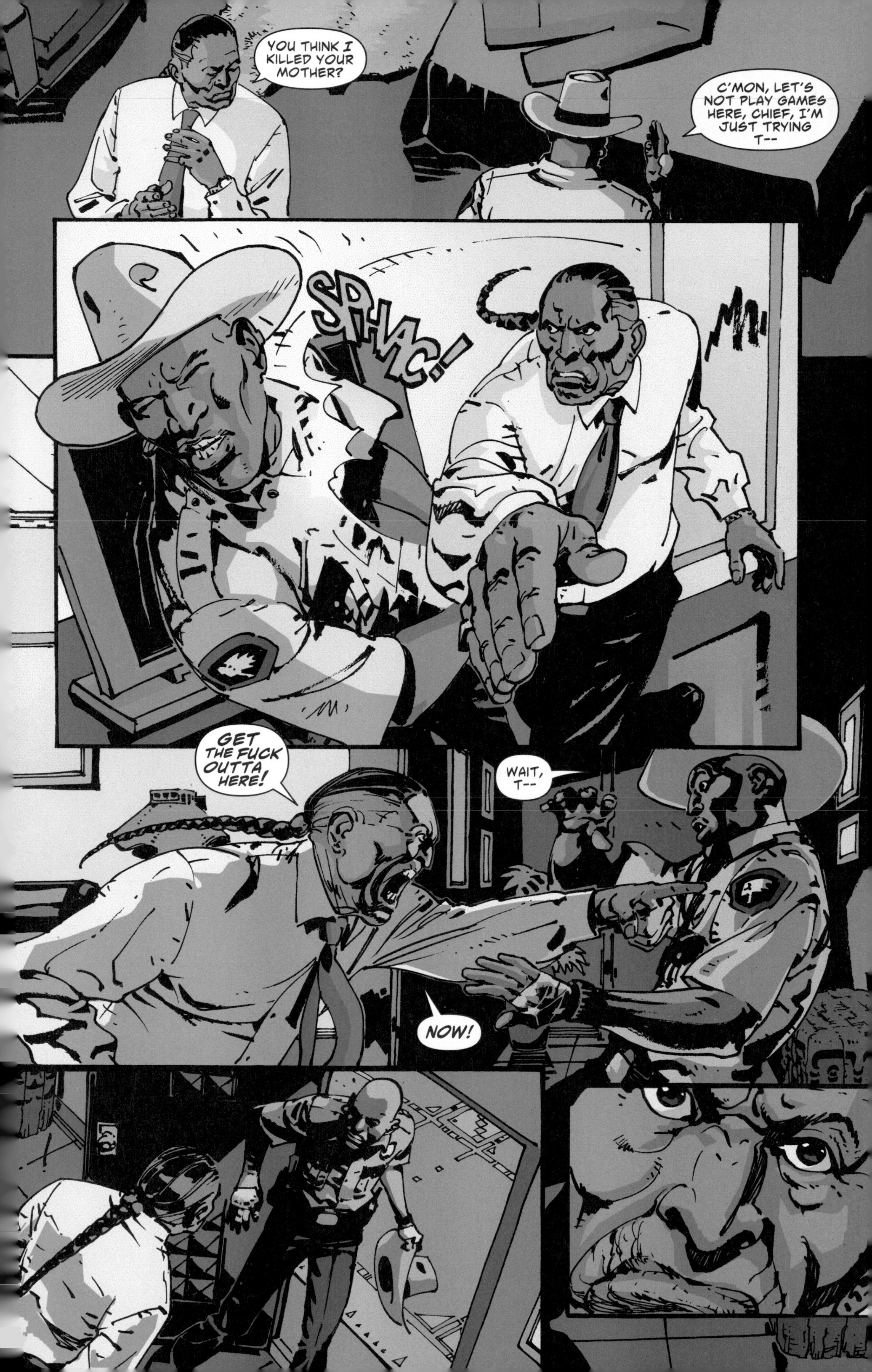
YOU THINK I KILLED YOUR MOTHER?
C'MON, LET'S NOT PLAY GAMES HERE, CHIEF, I'M JUST TRYING T--
SPHAC!
GET THE FUCK OUTTA HERE!
WAIT, T--
NOW!

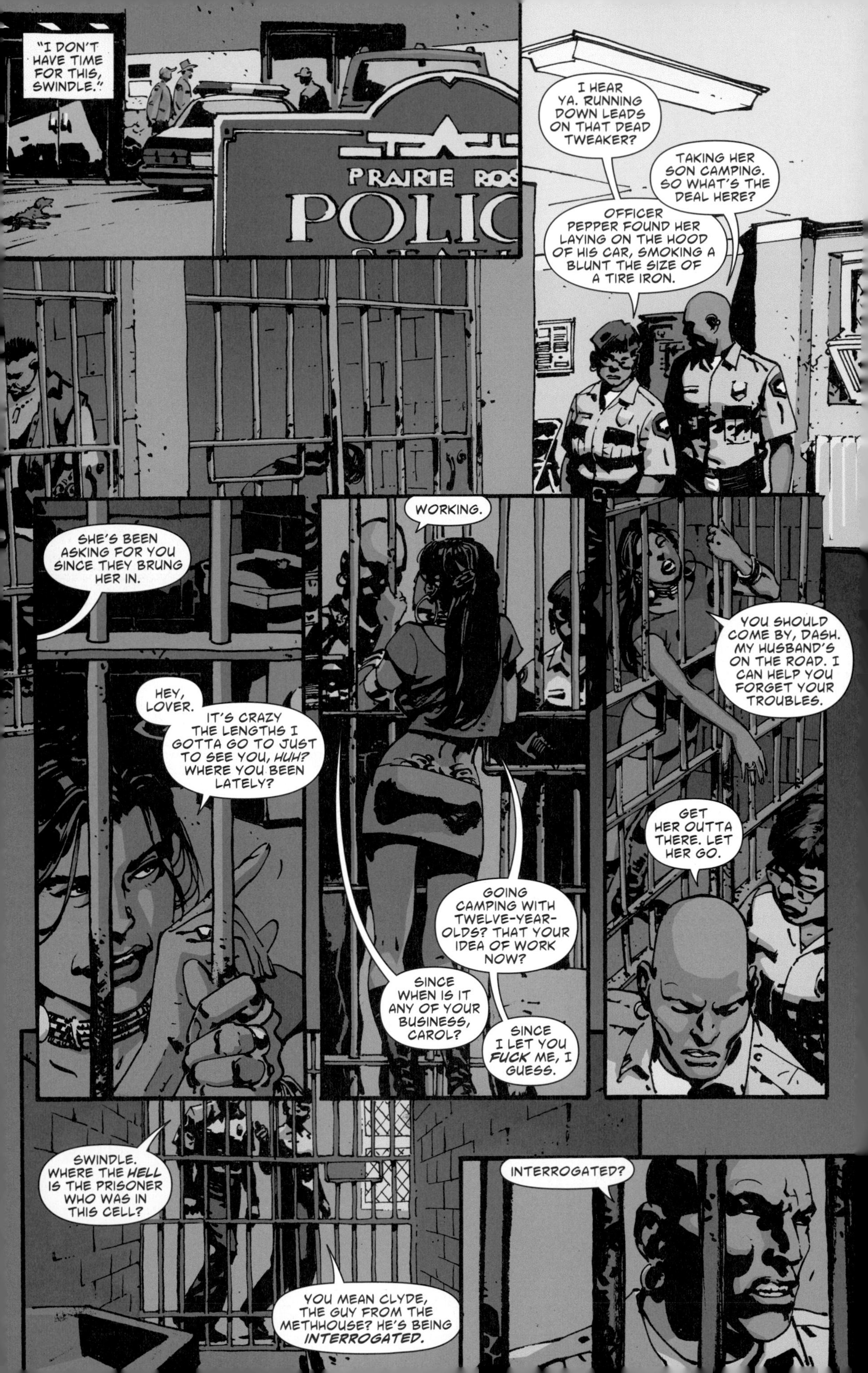
"I DON'T HAVE TIME FOR THIS, SWINDLE."
PRAIRIE ROS
POLIC
I HEAR YA. RUNNING DOWN LEADS ON THAT DEAD TWEAKER?
TAKING HER SON CAMPING. SO WHAT'S THE DEAL HERE?
OFFICER PEPPER FOUND HER LAYING ON THE HOOD OF HIS CAR, SMOKING A BLUNT THE SIZE OF A TIRE IRON.
SHE'S BEEN ASKING FOR YOU SINCE THEY BRUNG HER IN.
HEY, LOVER.
IT'S CRAZY THE LENGTHS I GOTTA GO TO JUST TO SEE YOU, HUH? WHERE YOU BEEN LATELY?
WORKING.
GOING CAMPING WITH TWELVE-YEAR-OLDS? THAT YOUR IDEA OF WORK NOW?
SINCE WHEN IS IT ANY OF YOUR BUSINESS, CAROL?
SINCE I LET YOU FUCK ME, I GUESS.
YOU SHOULD COME BY, DASH. MY HUSBAND'S ON THE ROAD. I CAN HELP YOU FORGET YOUR TROUBLES.
GET HER OUTTA THERE. LET HER GO.
SWINDLE. WHERE THE HELL IS THE PRISONER WHO WAS IN THIS CELL?
YOU MEAN CLYDE, THE GUY FROM THE METHHOUSE? HE'S BEING INTERROGATED.
INTERROGATED?

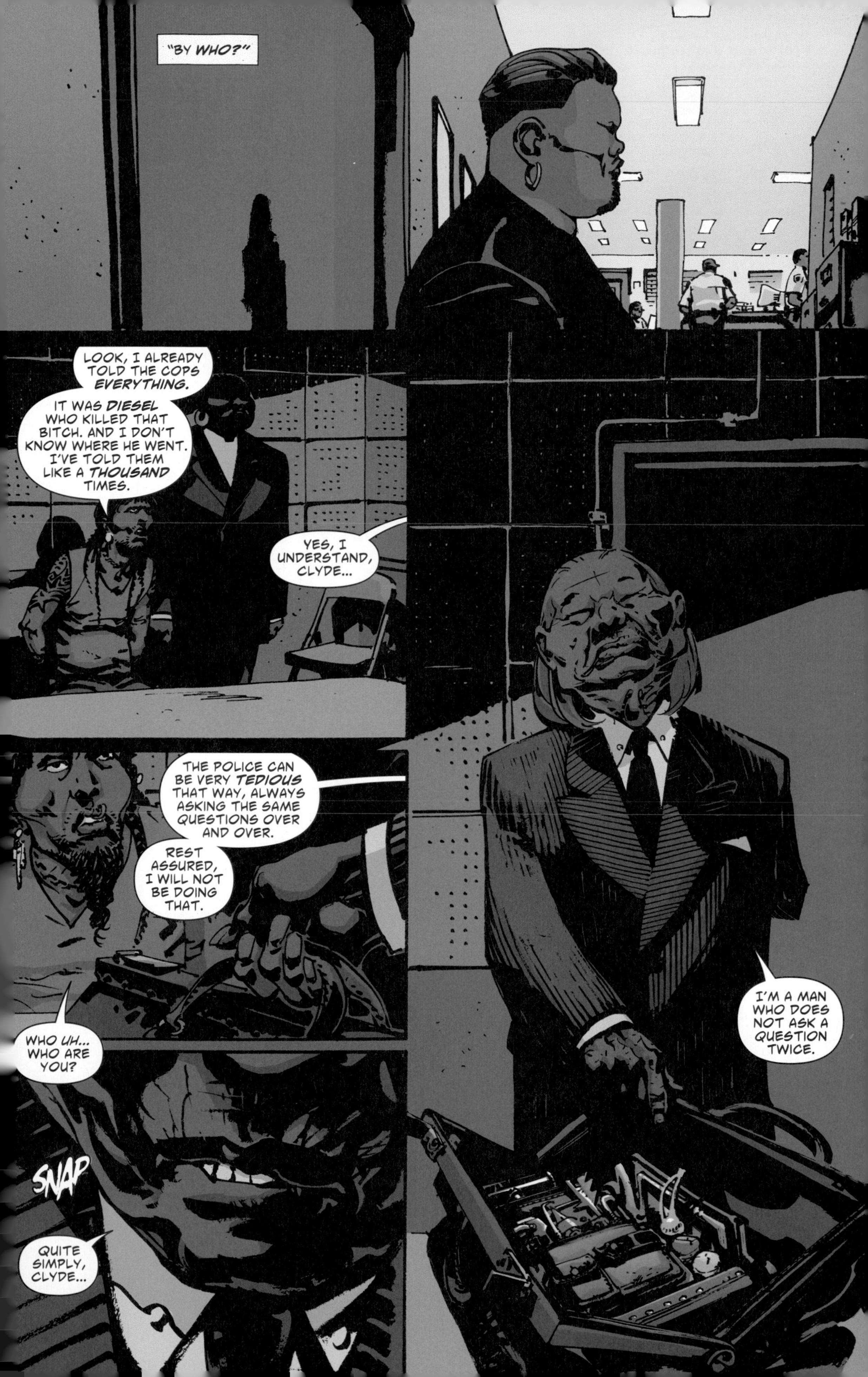
"BY WHO?"
LOOK, I ALREADY TOLD THE COPS EVERYTHING.
IT WAS DIESEL WHO KILLED THAT BITCH. AND I DON'T KNOW WHERE HE WENT. I'VE TOLD THEM LIKE A THOUSAND TIMES.
YES, I UNDERSTAND, CLYDE...
THE POLICE CAN BE VERY TEDIOUS THAT WAY, ALWAYS ASKING THE SAME QUESTIONS OVER AND OVER.
REST ASSURED, I WILL NOT BE DOING THAT.
WHO UH... WHO ARE YOU?
SNAP
QUITE SIMPLY, CLYDE...
I'M A MAN WHO DOES NOT ASK A QUESTION TWICE.

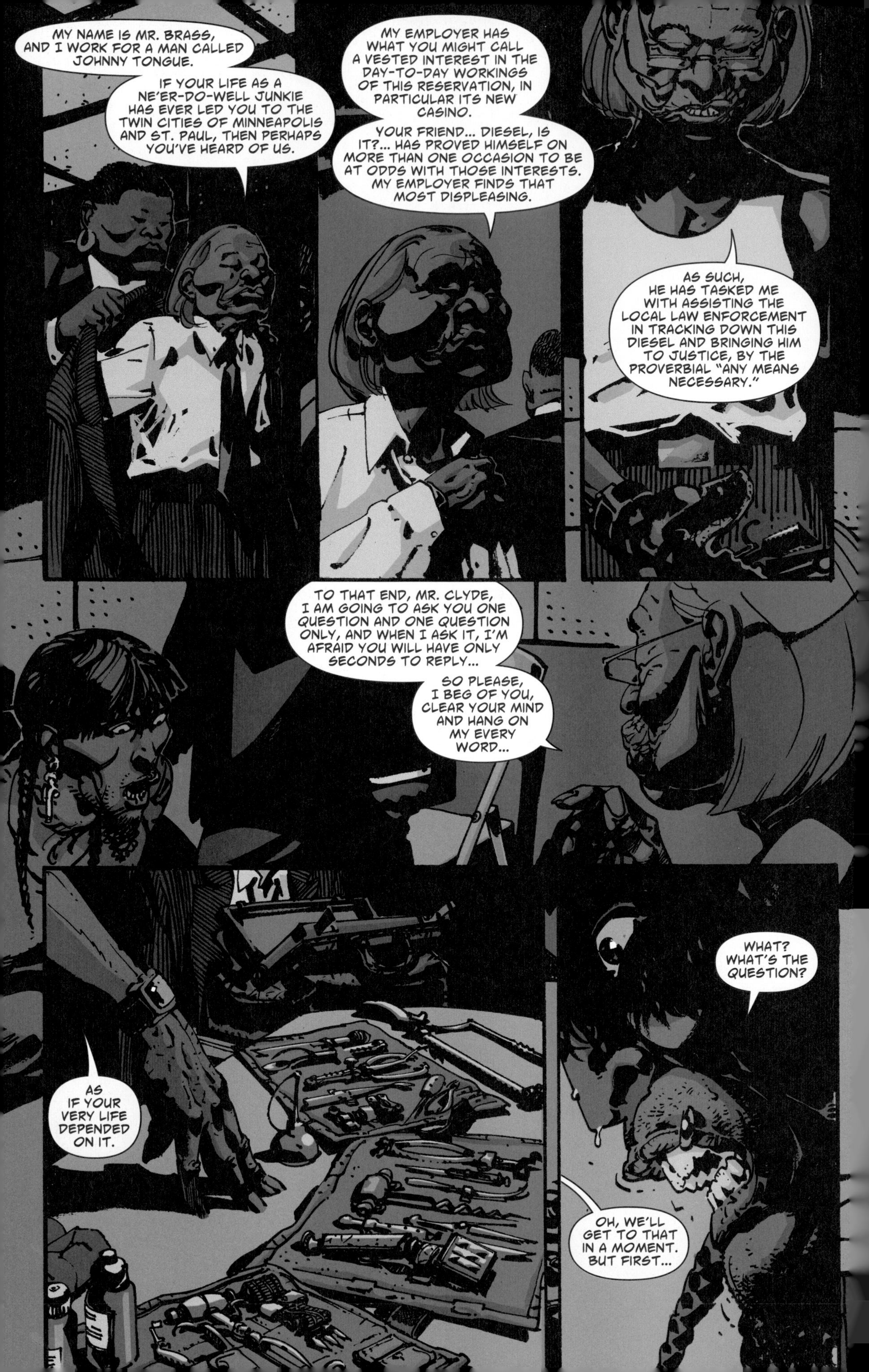
MY NAME IS MR. BRASS, AND I WORK FOR A MAN CALLED JOHNNY TONGUE.
IF YOUR LIFE AS A NE'ER-DO-WELL JUNKIE HAS EVER LED YOU TO THE TWIN CITIES OF MINNEAPOLIS AND ST. PAUL, THEN PERHAPS YOU'VE HEARD OF US.
MY EMPLOYER HAS WHAT YOU MIGHT CALL A VESTED INTEREST IN THE DAY-TO-DAY WORKINGS OF THIS RESERVATION, IN PARTICULAR ITS NEW CASINO.
YOUR FRIEND... DIESEL, IS IT?... HAS PROVED HIMSELF ON MORE THAN ONE OCCASION TO BE AT ODDS WITH THOSE INTERESTS. MY EMPLOYER FINDS THAT MOST DISPLEASING.
AS SUCH, HE HAS TASKED ME WITH ASSISTING THE LOCAL LAW ENFORCEMENT IN TRACKING DOWN THIS DIESEL AND BRINGING HIM TO JUSTICE, BY THE PROVERBIAL "ANY MEANS NECESSARY."
TO THAT END, MR. CLYDE, I AM GOING TO ASK YOU ONE QUESTION AND ONE QUESTION ONLY, AND WHEN I ASK IT, I'M AFRAID YOU WILL HAVE ONLY SECONDS TO REPLY...
SO PLEASE, I BEG OF YOU, CLEAR YOUR MIND AND HANG ON MY EVERY WORD...
AS IF YOUR VERY LIFE DEPENDED ON IT.
WHAT? WHAT'S THE QUESTION?
OH, WE'LL GET TO THAT IN A MOMENT. BUT FIRST...

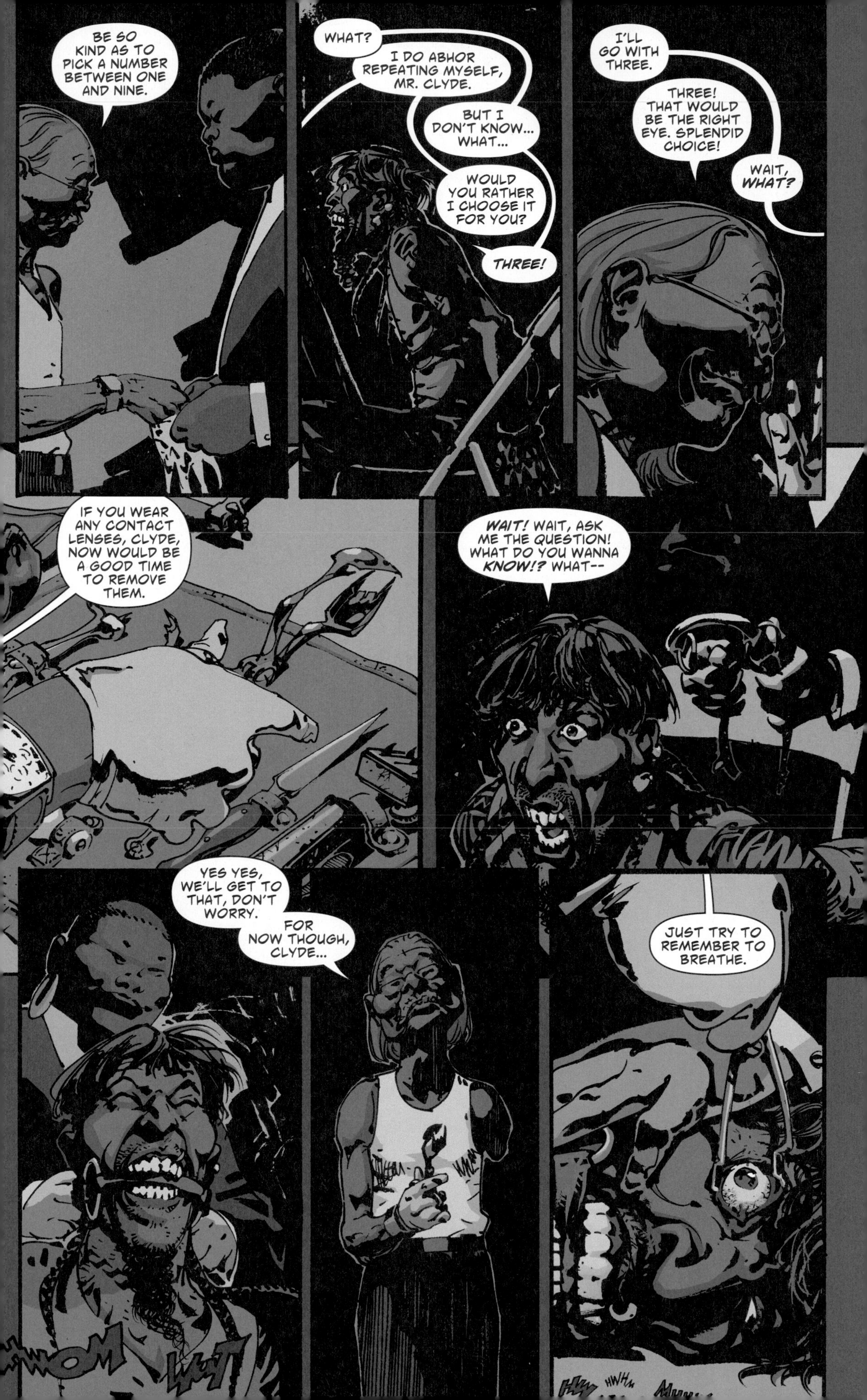
BE SO KIND AS TO PICK A NUMBER BETWEEN ONE AND NINE.
WHAT?
I DO ABHOR REPEATING MYSELF, MR. CLYDE.
BUT I DON'T KNOW... WHAT...
WOULD YOU RATHER I CHOOSE IT FOR YOU?
THREE!
I'LL GO WITH THREE.
THREE! THAT WOULD BE THE RIGHT EYE. SPLENDID CHOICE!
WAIT, WHAT?
IF YOU WEAR ANY CONTACT LENSES, CLYDE, NOW WOULD BE A GOOD TIME TO REMOVE THEM.
WAIT! WAIT, ASK ME THE QUESTION! WHAT DO YOU WANNA KNOW!? WHAT--
YES YES, WE'LL GET TO THAT, DON'T WORRY.
FOR NOW THOUGH, CLYDE...
JUST TRY TO REMEMBER TO BREATHE.

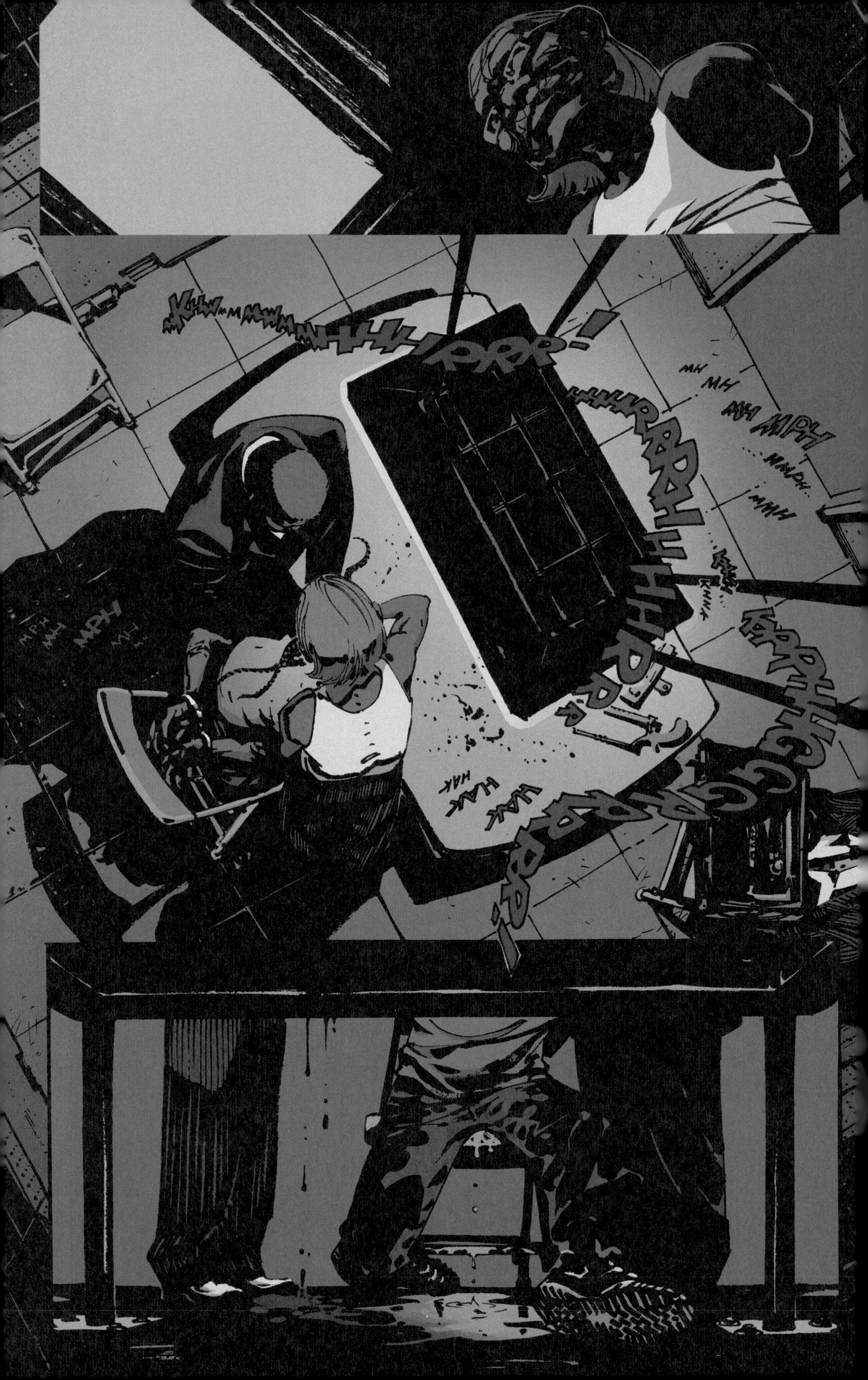
KHWMMMWMMHHHHIPRRR-!
MH MH MH MPH
...MMPH...
MMH
HAK HAK HAK

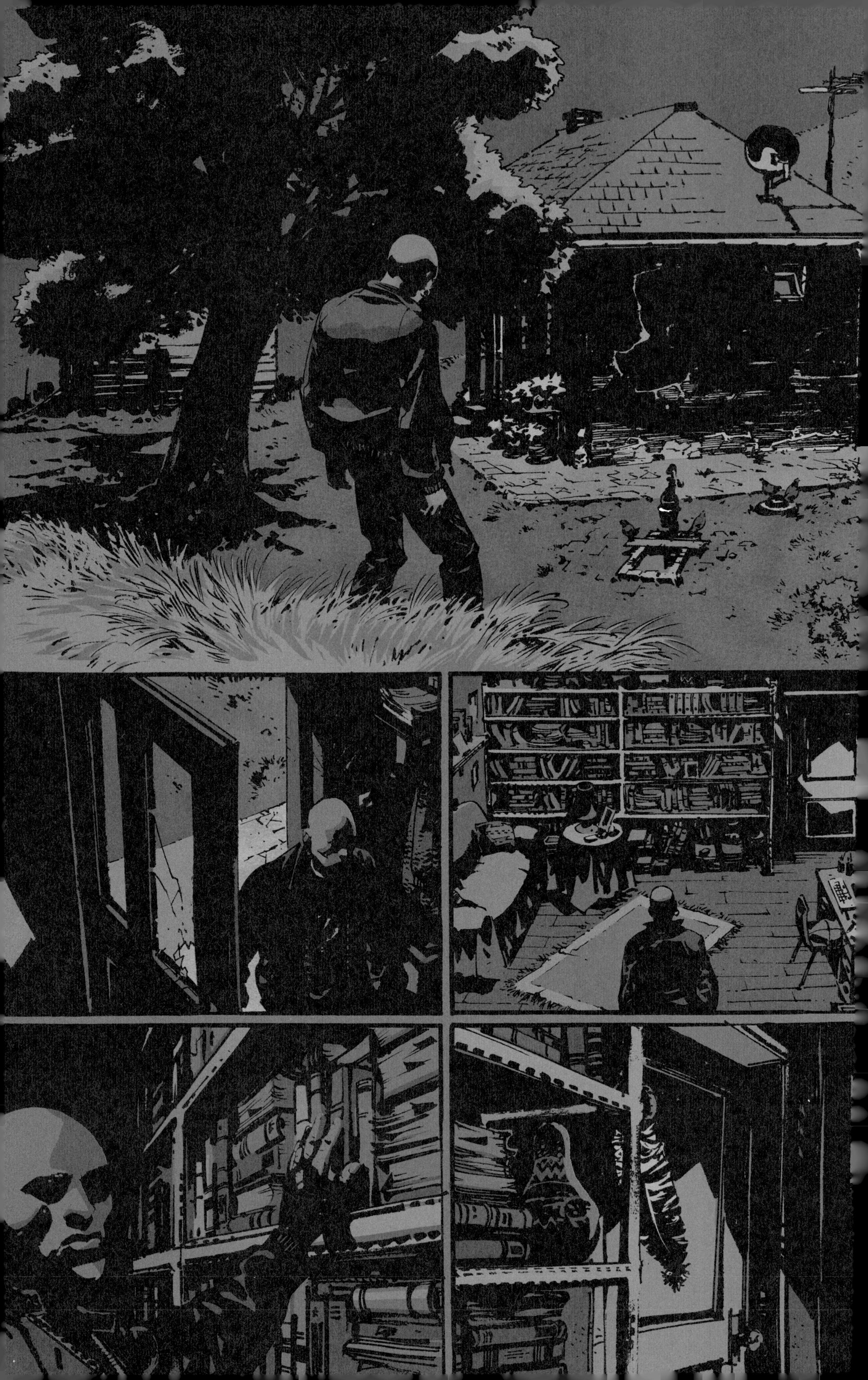

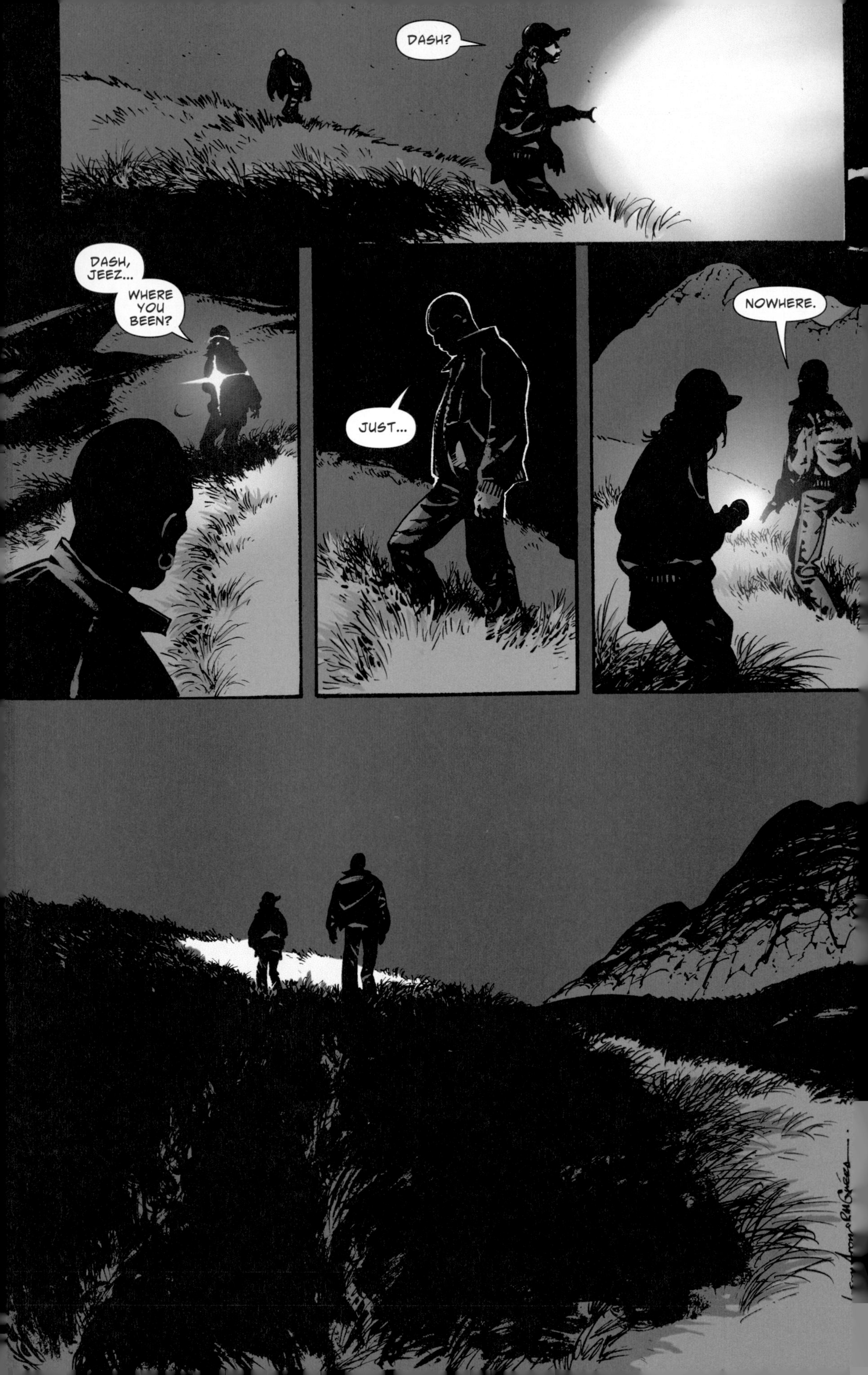
DASH?
DASH, JEEZ...
WHERE YOU BEEN?
JUST...
NOWHERE.

YOU TURN OVER EVERYTHING YOU'VE GOT ON THIS SUSPECT TO ME, AND I'LL SEE WHAT I CAN DO ABOUT TRACKING HIM DOWN FOR YOU.

THAT WAY, YOU CAN DEVOTE ALL YOUR RESOURCES TO FINDING WHOEVER KILLED GINA BAD HORSE. THAT'S WHAT YOU *REALLY* WANNA BE DOING, RIGHT?

I MEAN, SHE WAS A RESPECTED TRIBAL LEADER AND ALL. NOT TO MENTION THE FACT THAT YOU TWO WERE SUCH GOOD PALS.

I BET YOU JUST CAN'T REST UNTIL HER KILLER'S BROUGHT TO JUSTICE. RIGHT?

DON'T TELL ME HOW TO RUN MY AFFAIRS.

I'LL TELL YOU WHATEVER I GODDAMN WELL PLEASE, LINCOLN.

YOU DON'T LIKE IT...

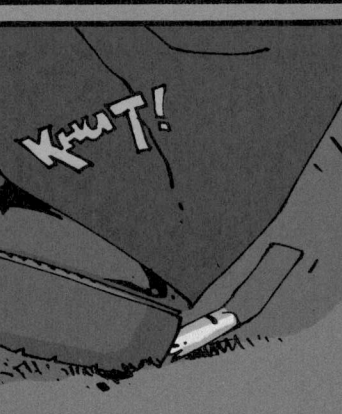

K-HT!

GO TELL YOUR ANCESTORS THEY SHOULDN'T A' SIGNED ALL THEM FUCKING TREATIES.

YOUR MOTHER WOULD WANT YOU WITH YOUR FAMILY. SHE'D WANT YOU THERE TO LOOK AFTER YOUR BROTHERS AND SISTERS.

AND WE'LL KEEP LOOKING, SHELTON, I *PROMISE* YOU. WE'LL KEEP LOOKING UNTIL WE FIND THE BASTARD.

I HEAR HE'S HIDING OUT IN NEBRASKA NOW.

WHERE'D YOU HEAR THAT?

'S WHAT EVERYBODY SAYS.

WHAT *ELSE* DO THEY SAY?

SHELTON?

THANKS FOR HANGING OUT WITH ME THE LAST FEW DAYS. SHOWING ME AROUND. TEACHING ME HOW TO SHOOT AND ALL.

YEAH, IT WAS, *UH...* YOU KNOW... IT WAS *COOL*.

I BETTER BE GOING.

HEY, HOLD UP. I GOT SOMETHING FOR YOU.

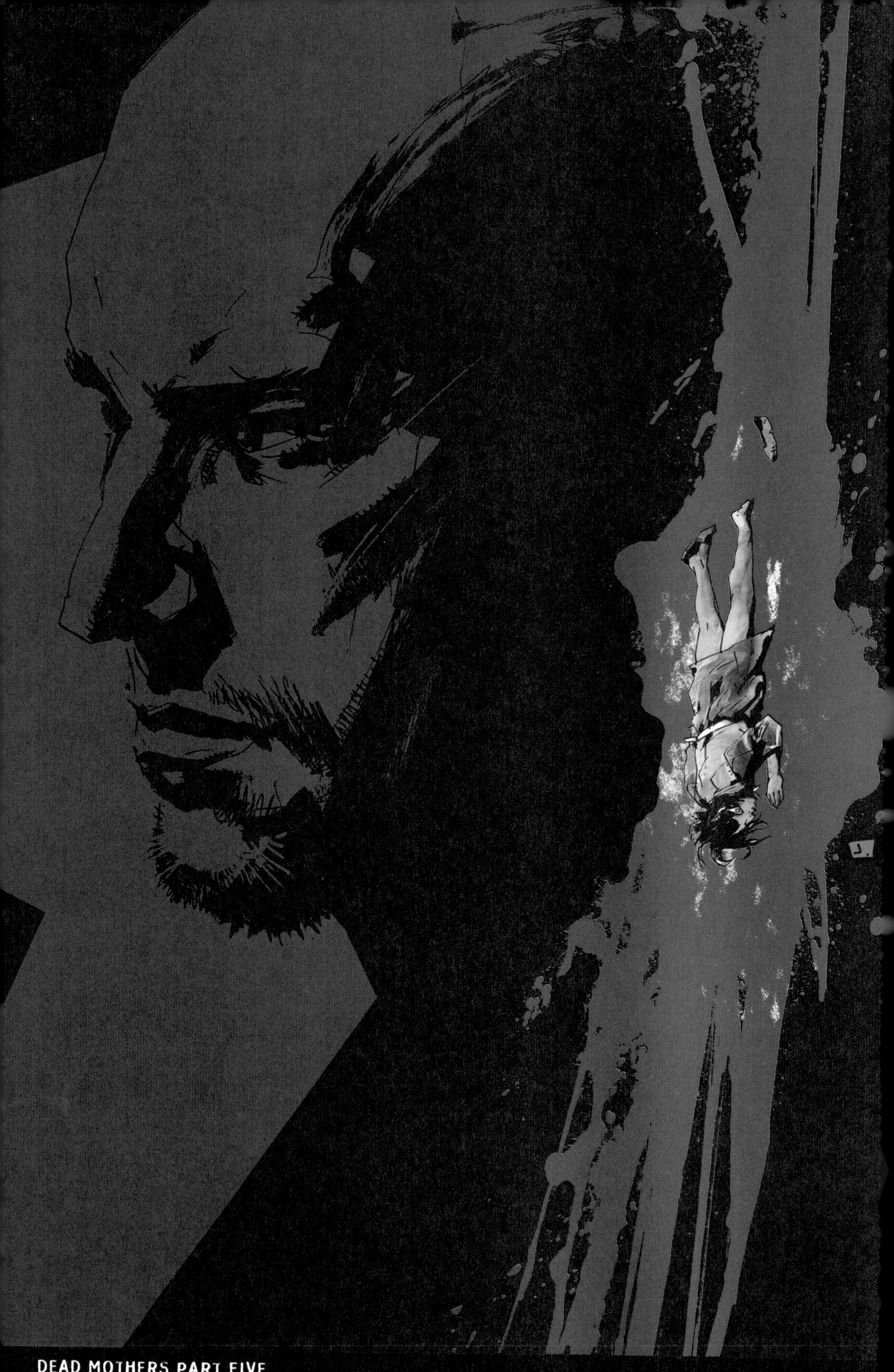

DEAD MOTHERS PART FIVE

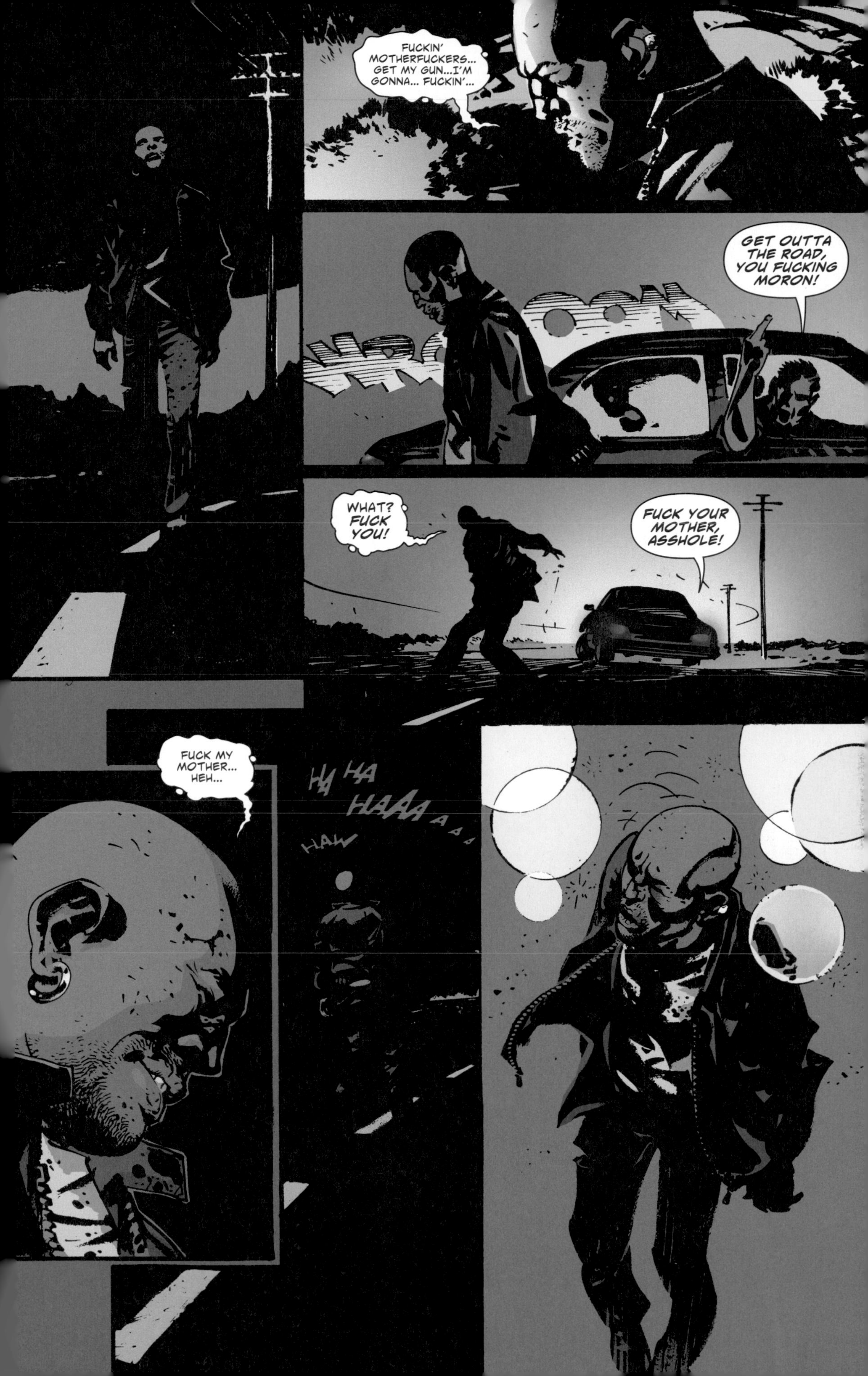

FUCKIN' MOTHERFUCKERS... GET MY GUN...I'M GONNA... FUCKIN'...
GET OUTTA THE ROAD, YOU FUCKING MORON!
WHAT? FUCK YOU!
FUCK YOUR MOTHER, ASSHOLE!
FUCK MY MOTHER... HEH...
HA HA HAAA A A A
HAW

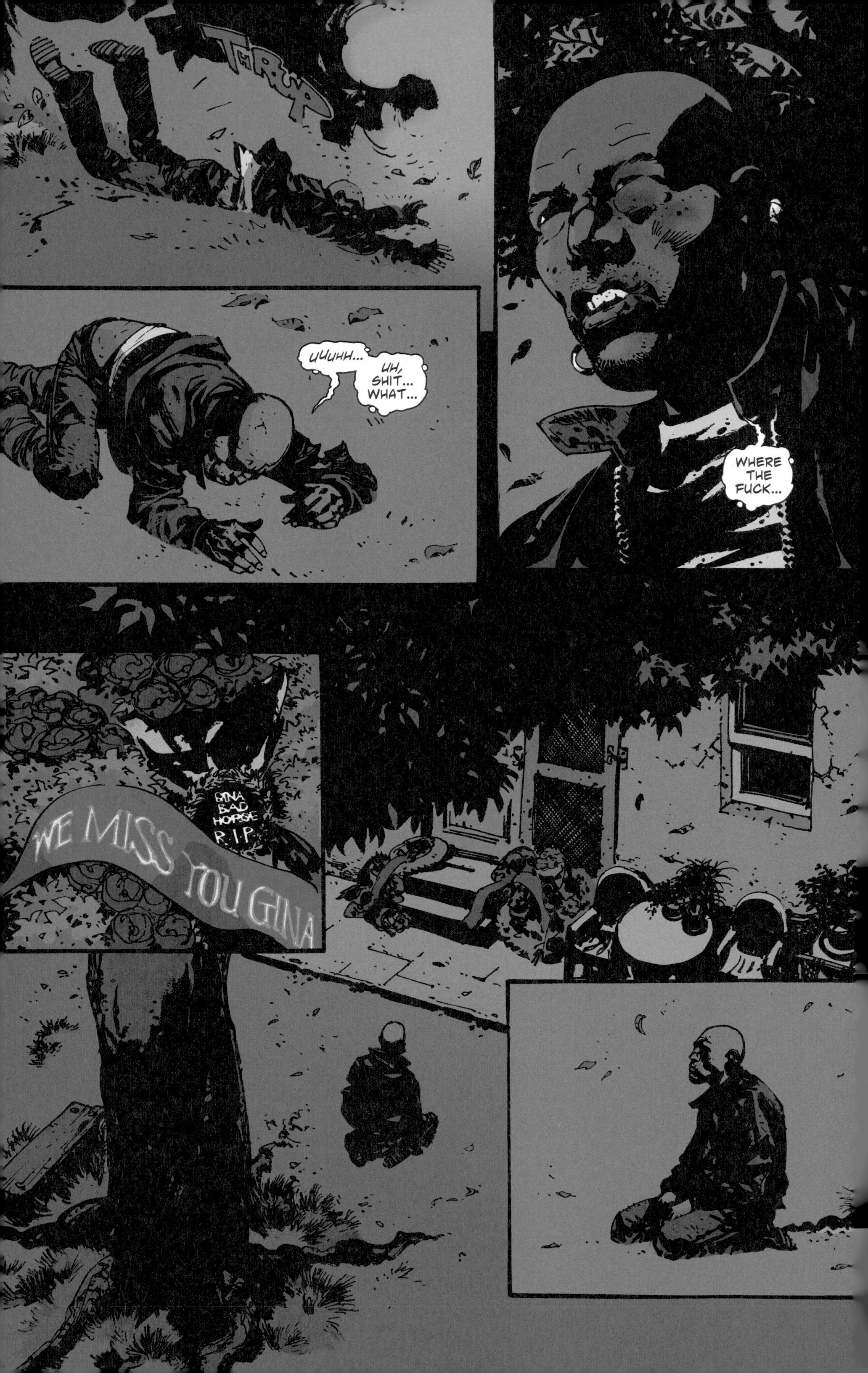
THRUP
UUUHH...
UH, SHIT... WHAT...
WHERE THE FUCK...
GINA BAD HORSE R.I.P.
WE MISS YOU GINA

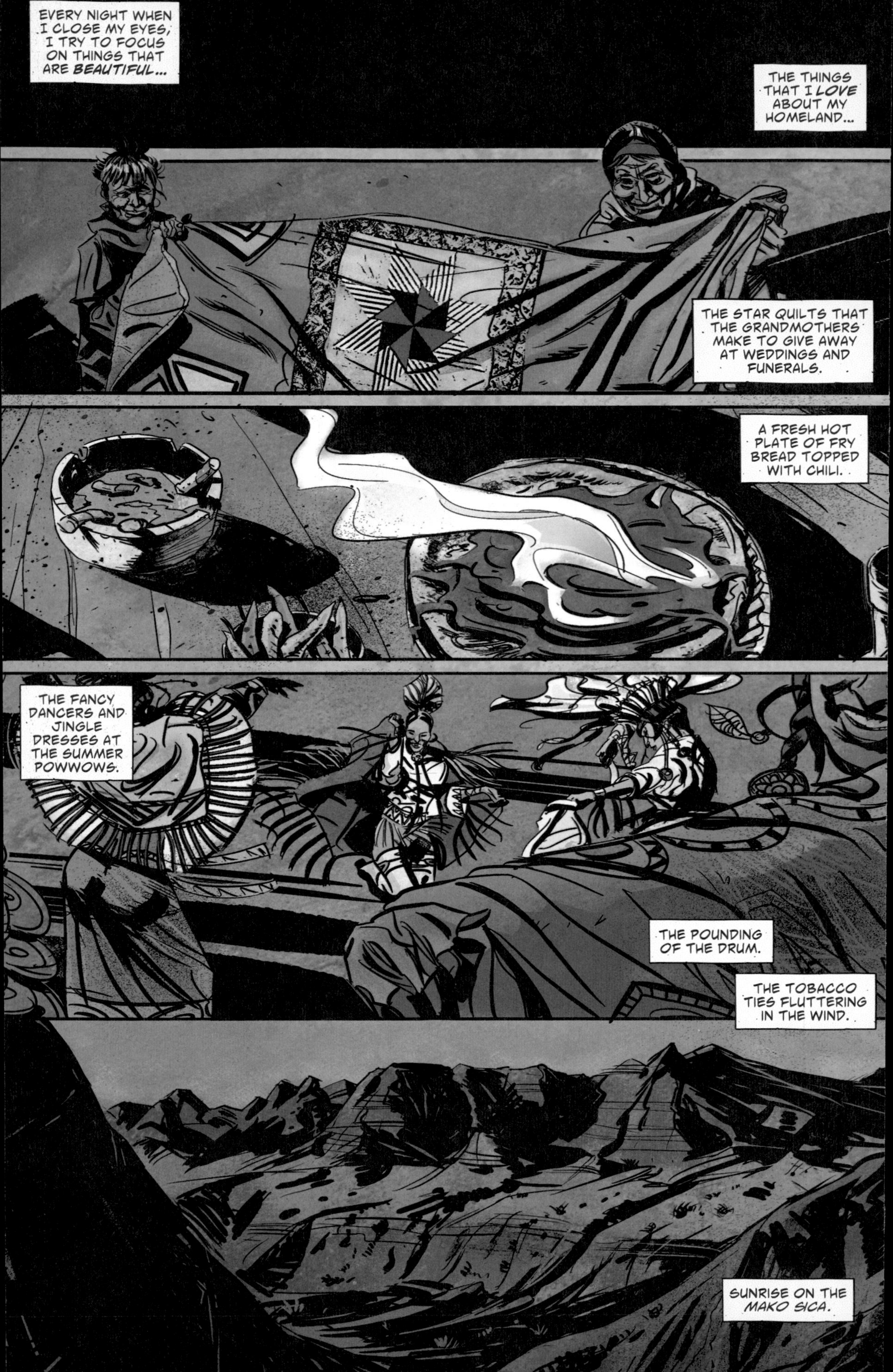
EVERY NIGHT WHEN I CLOSE MY EYES, I TRY TO FOCUS ON THINGS THAT ARE *BEAUTIFUL*...
THE THINGS THAT I *LOVE* ABOUT MY HOMELAND...
THE STAR QUILTS THAT THE GRANDMOTHERS MAKE TO GIVE AWAY AT WEDDINGS AND FUNERALS.
A FRESH HOT PLATE OF FRY BREAD TOPPED WITH CHILI.
THE FANCY DANCERS AND JINGLE DRESSES AT THE SUMMER POWWOWS.
THE POUNDING OF THE DRUM.
THE TOBACCO TIES FLUTTERING IN THE WIND.
SUNRISE ON THE *MAKO SICA*.

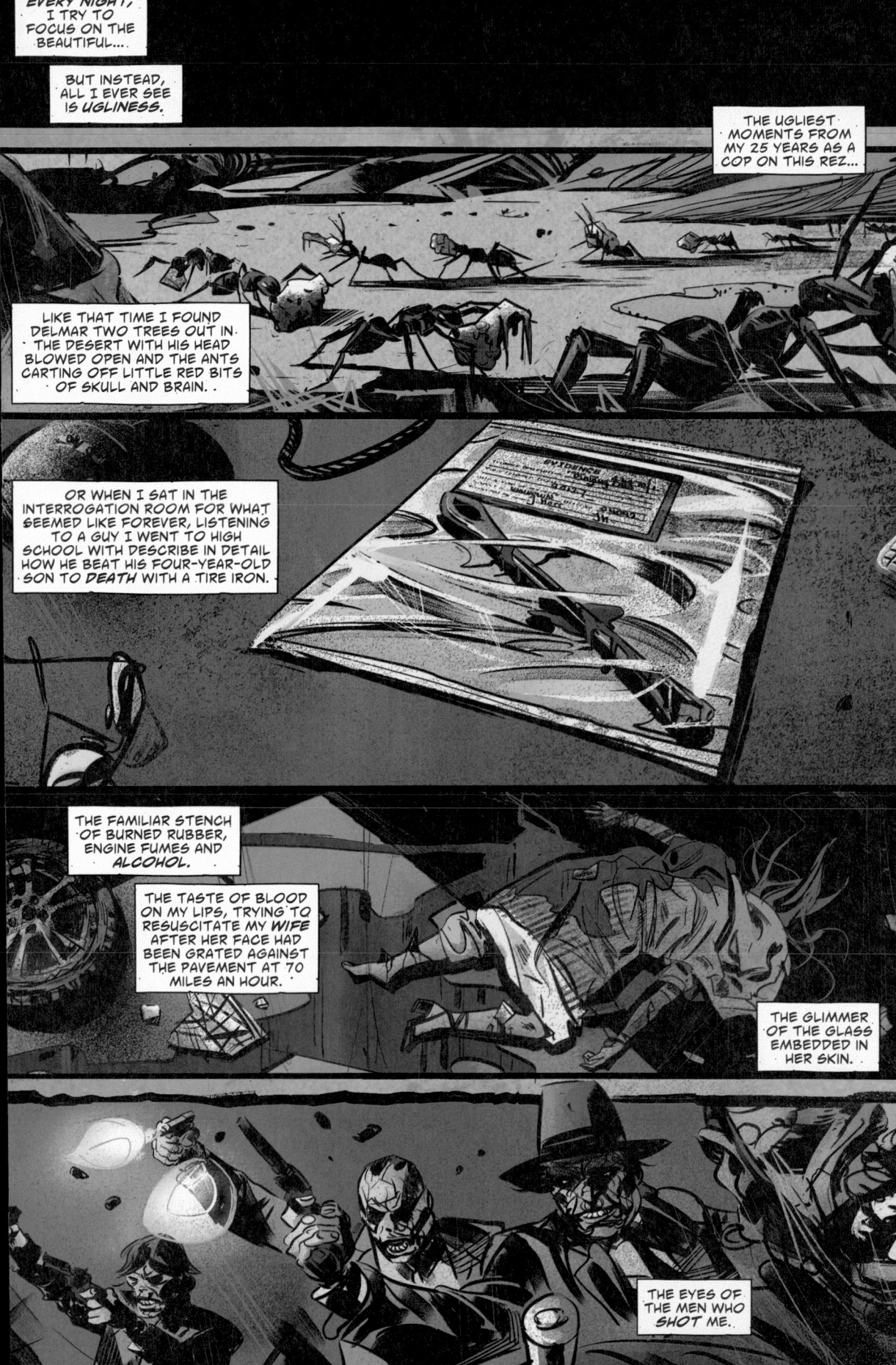

EVERY NIGHT, I TRY TO FOCUS ON THE BEAUTIFUL....

BUT INSTEAD, ALL I EVER SEE IS *UGLINESS*.

THE UGLIEST MOMENTS FROM MY 25 YEARS AS A COP ON THIS REZ...

LIKE THAT TIME I FOUND DELMAR TWO TREES OUT IN THE DESERT WITH HIS HEAD BLOWED OPEN AND THE ANTS CARTING OFF LITTLE RED BITS OF SKULL AND BRAIN.

OR WHEN I SAT IN THE INTERROGATION ROOM FOR WHAT SEEMED LIKE FOREVER, LISTENING TO A GUY I WENT TO HIGH SCHOOL WITH DESCRIBE IN DETAIL HOW HE BEAT HIS FOUR-YEAR-OLD SON TO *DEATH* WITH A TIRE IRON.

THE FAMILIAR STENCH OF BURNED RUBBER, ENGINE FUMES AND *ALCOHOL*.

THE TASTE OF BLOOD ON MY LIPS, TRYING TO RESUSCITATE MY *WIFE* AFTER HER FACE HAD BEEN GRATED AGAINST THE PAVEMENT AT 70 MILES AN HOUR.

THE GLIMMER OF THE GLASS EMBEDDED IN HER SKIN.

THE EYES OF THE MEN WHO *SHOT* ME.

MY NAME IS *FRANKLIN FALLS DOWN*, OFFICER OF THE PRAIRIE ROSE TRIBAL POLICE FORCE.

AND I KNOW PRETTY MUCH *EVERYTHING* THERE IS TO KNOW ABOUT BEING A *COP* IN INDIAN COUNTRY.

I KNOW WHICH KIDS SELL WEED AND WHICH ONES SMOKE IT. I KNOW HOW TO SPOT A METH HOUSE FROM A MILE AWAY. HOW TO TELL IF A SUSPECT'S CARRYING A CONCEALED WEAPON BY THE WAY HE WALKS.

I KNOW HOW TO TRACK A MAN ACROSS OPEN GROUND FROM HORSEBACK AND HOW TO JUDGE HOW LONG A BODY'S BEEN IN THE SUN BY WHAT THE COYOTES HAVE DONE TO IT.

THE ONE THING I AIN'T NEVER BEEN SO GOOD AT IS *LETTING GO.*

THOUGH MAYBE IT'S HIGH PAST TIME I LEARNED.

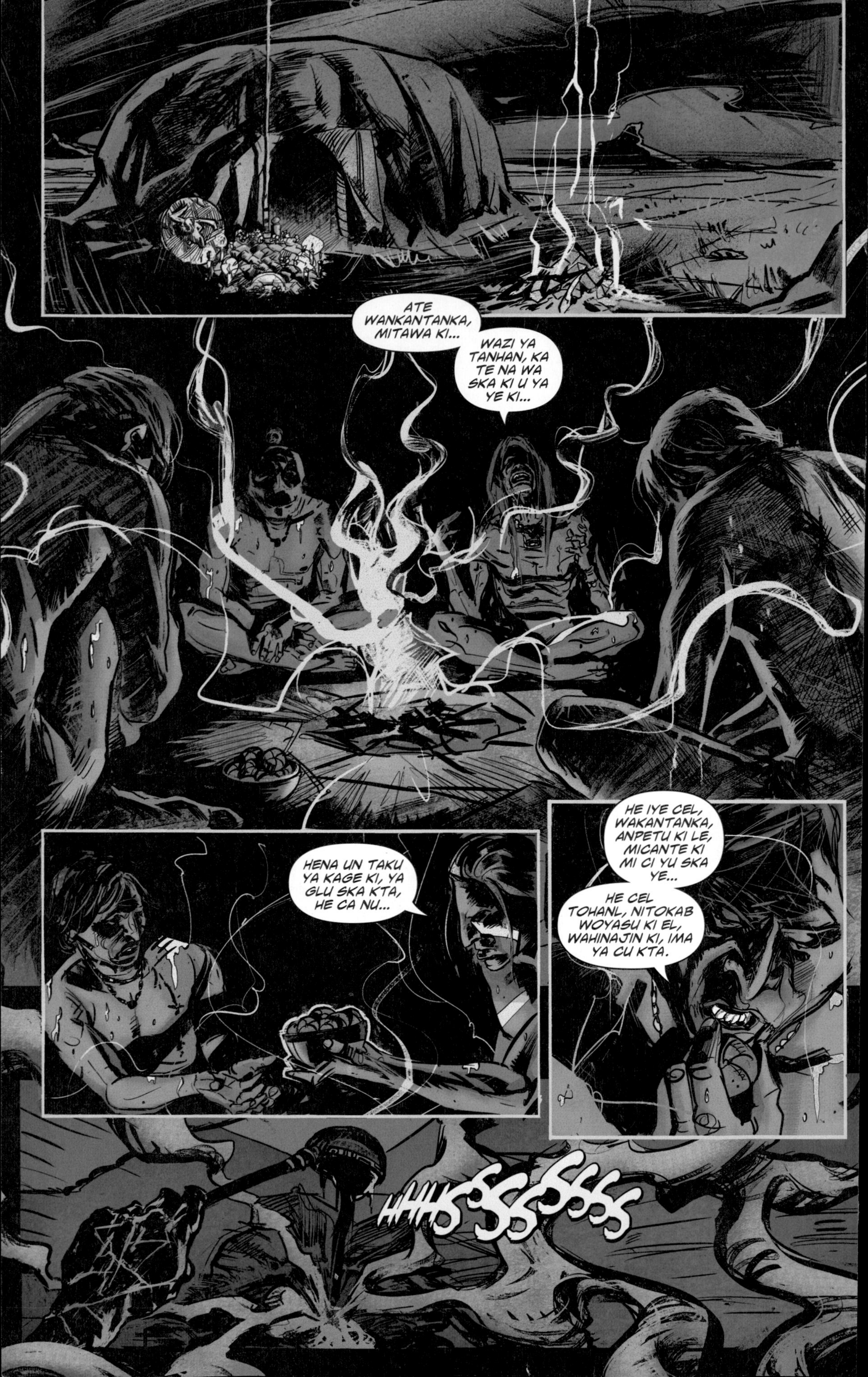

ATE WANKANTANKA, MITAWA KI...
WAZI YA TANHAN, KA TE NA WA SKA KI U YA YE KI...
HENA UN TAKU YA KAGE KI, YA GLU SKA KTA, HE CA NU...
HE IYE CEL, WAKANTANKA, ANPETU KI LE, MICANTE KI MI CI YU SKA YE...
HE CEL TOHANL, NITOKAB WOYASU KI EL, WAHINAJIN KI, IMA YA CU KTA.
HHHSSSSSSSSS

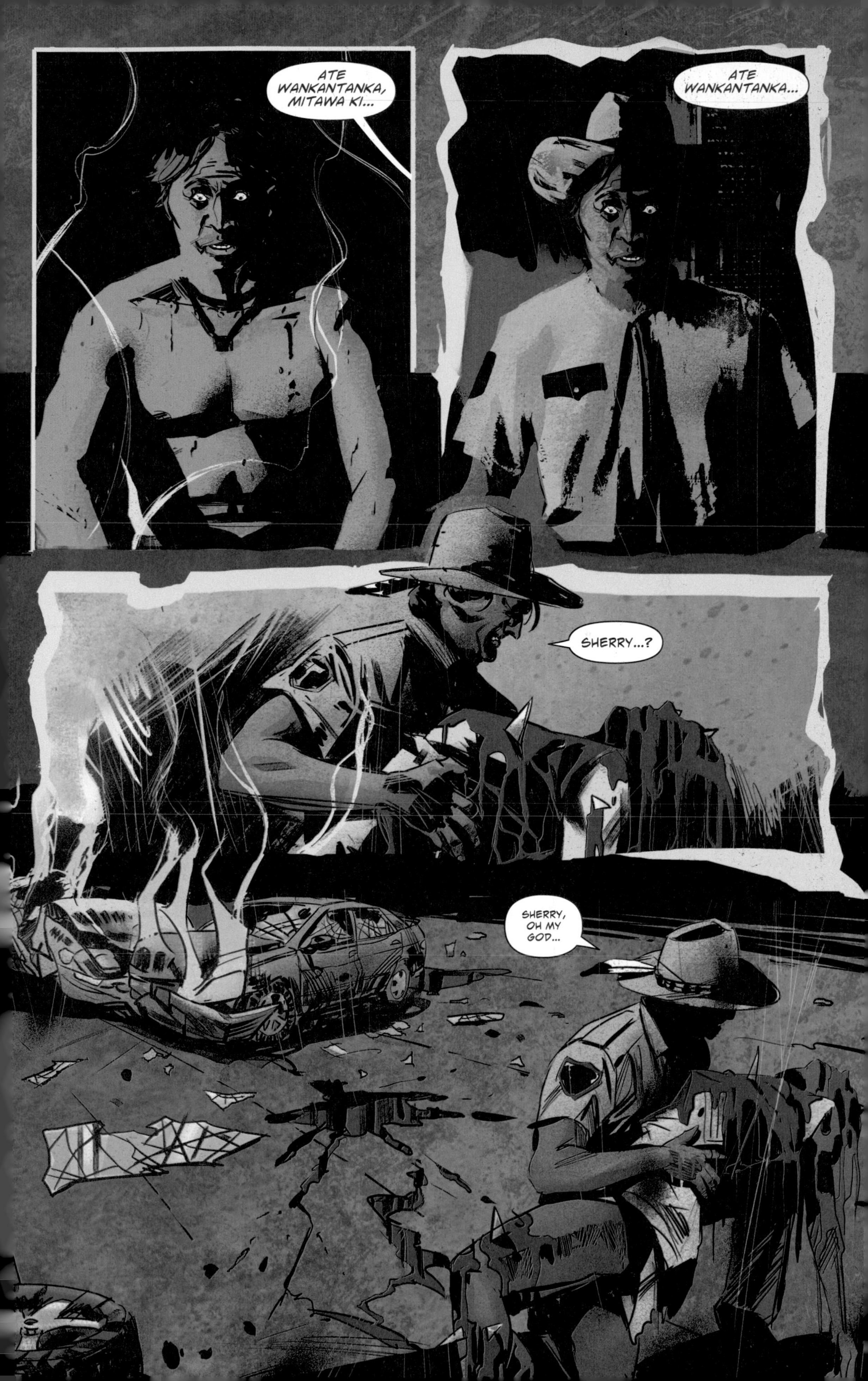
ATE WANKANTANKA, MITAWA KI...
ATE WANKANTANKA...
SHERRY...?
SHERRY, OH MY GOD...

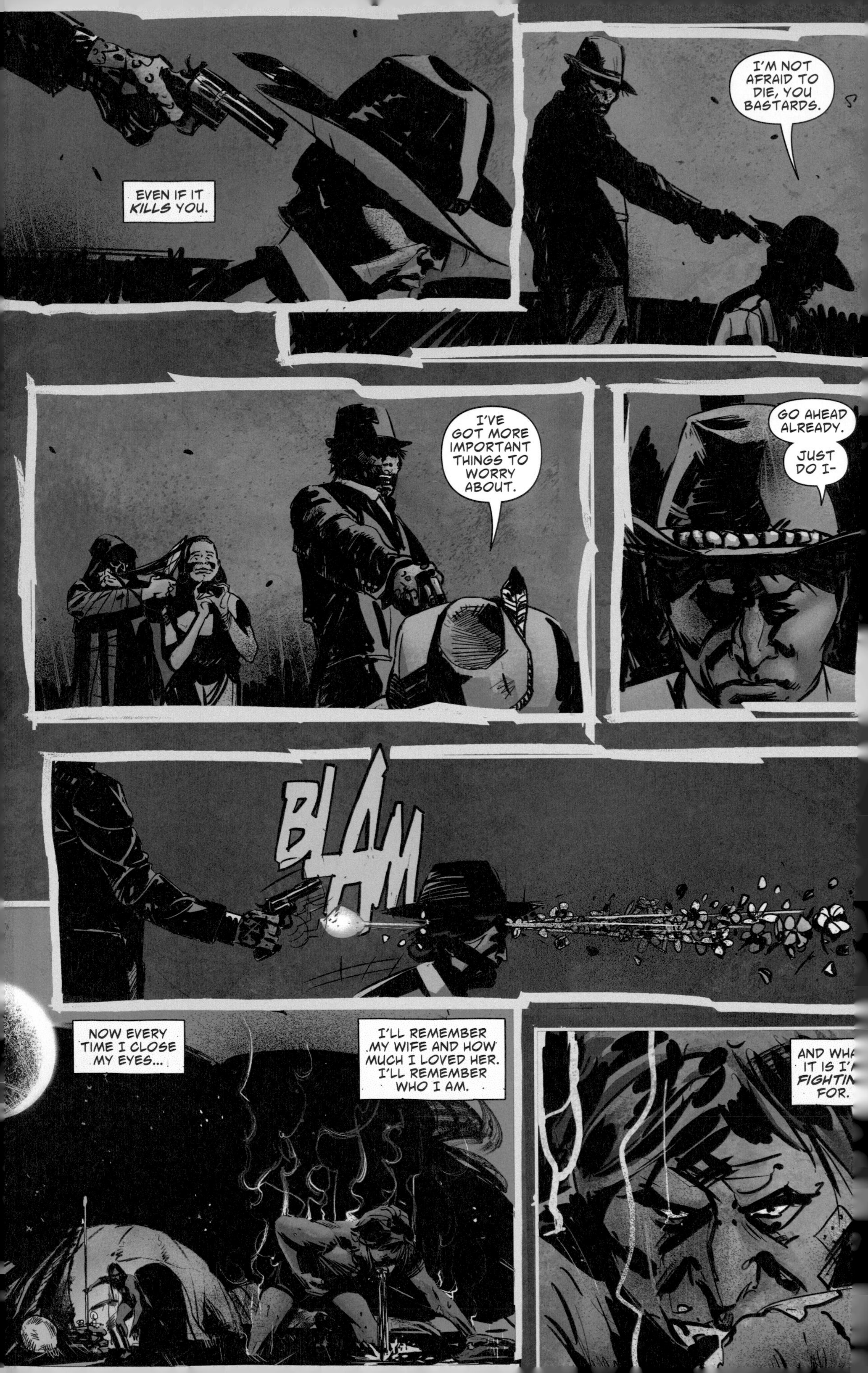
EVEN IF IT *KILLS* YOU.
I'M NOT AFRAID TO DIE, YOU BASTARDS.
I'VE GOT MORE IMPORTANT THINGS TO WORRY ABOUT.
GO AHEAD ALREADY.
JUST DO I-
BLAM
NOW EVERY TIME I CLOSE MY EYES...
I'LL REMEMBER MY WIFE AND HOW MUCH I LOVED HER. I'LL REMEMBER WHO I AM.
AND WHA IT IS I'/ FIGHTIN FOR.

O'RAY!

O'RAY BEAVER, COME ON OUT, SON!

THIS IS OFFICER FALLS DOWN. YOU KNOW... THE GUY YOU PUNCHED IN THE FACE AND STOLE HIS GUN.

O'RAY, YOU IN THERE?!

THAT'S FAR ENOUGH, PIG.

THAT'S *MY* GUN.

YEAH? WELL, PUT YOUR DAMN HANDS UP, 'LESS YA WANNA GET *SHOT* WITH IT.

YOU AIN'T GONNA SHOOT ME, KID.

NEXT ONE GOES BETWEEN YOUR EYES.

NOW PUT YOUR DAMN HANDS UP.

LET ME TELL YOU WHAT'S ABOUT TO HAPPEN, SON. YOU'RE GONNA GIVE ME BACK MY GUN. AND THEN YOU'RE GONNA TURN YOURSELF IN. AND YOU 'N ME ARE GONNA DRIVE ON BACK TO THE POLICE STATION *TOGETHER*.

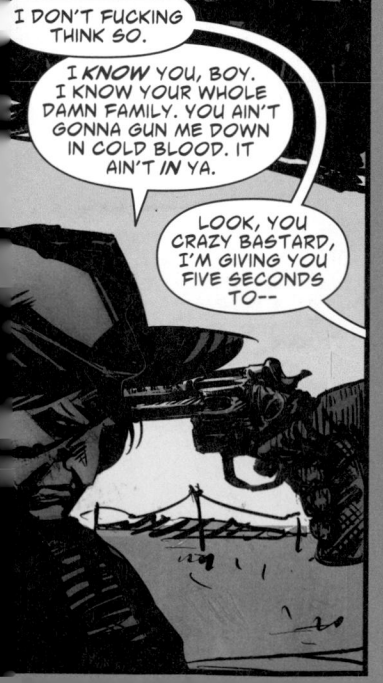

I DON'T FUCKING THINK SO.

I *KNOW* YOU, BOY. I KNOW YOUR WHOLE DAMN FAMILY. YOU AIN'T GONNA GUN ME DOWN IN COLD BLOOD. IT AIN'T *IN* YA.

LOOK, YOU CRAZY BASTARD, I'M GIVING YOU FIVE SECONDS TO--

FIVE SECONDS'LL BE JUST FINE.

FIVE SECONDS FROM NOW, EITHER YOU HAND OVER THAT GUN, O'RAY...

OR YOU *USE* IT.

I'M INVESTIGATING THE DEATH OF *GINA BAD HORSE.* AND YOU WERE THE LAST KNOWN PERSON TO SEE HER ALIVE.

SEEMS LIKE WE'VE GOT A LOT TO TALK ABOUT, MR. BELCOURT.

IF YOU'RE FROM PRAIRIE ROSE THEN YOU'RE ONE OF *RED CROW'S.* AND THAT MEANS I GOT *NOTHING* TO SAY TO YOU, PAL.

I DON'T GIVE A DAMN ABOUT RED CROW OR HIS INTERESTS. ALL I CARE ABOUT IS FINDING GINA'S MURDERER. ALL I WANT IS THE *TRUTH.* WHY DON'T WE START WITH THAT.

TELL ME *EVERYTHING.*

OKAY.

END.

THE BOUDOIR STOMP PART ONE

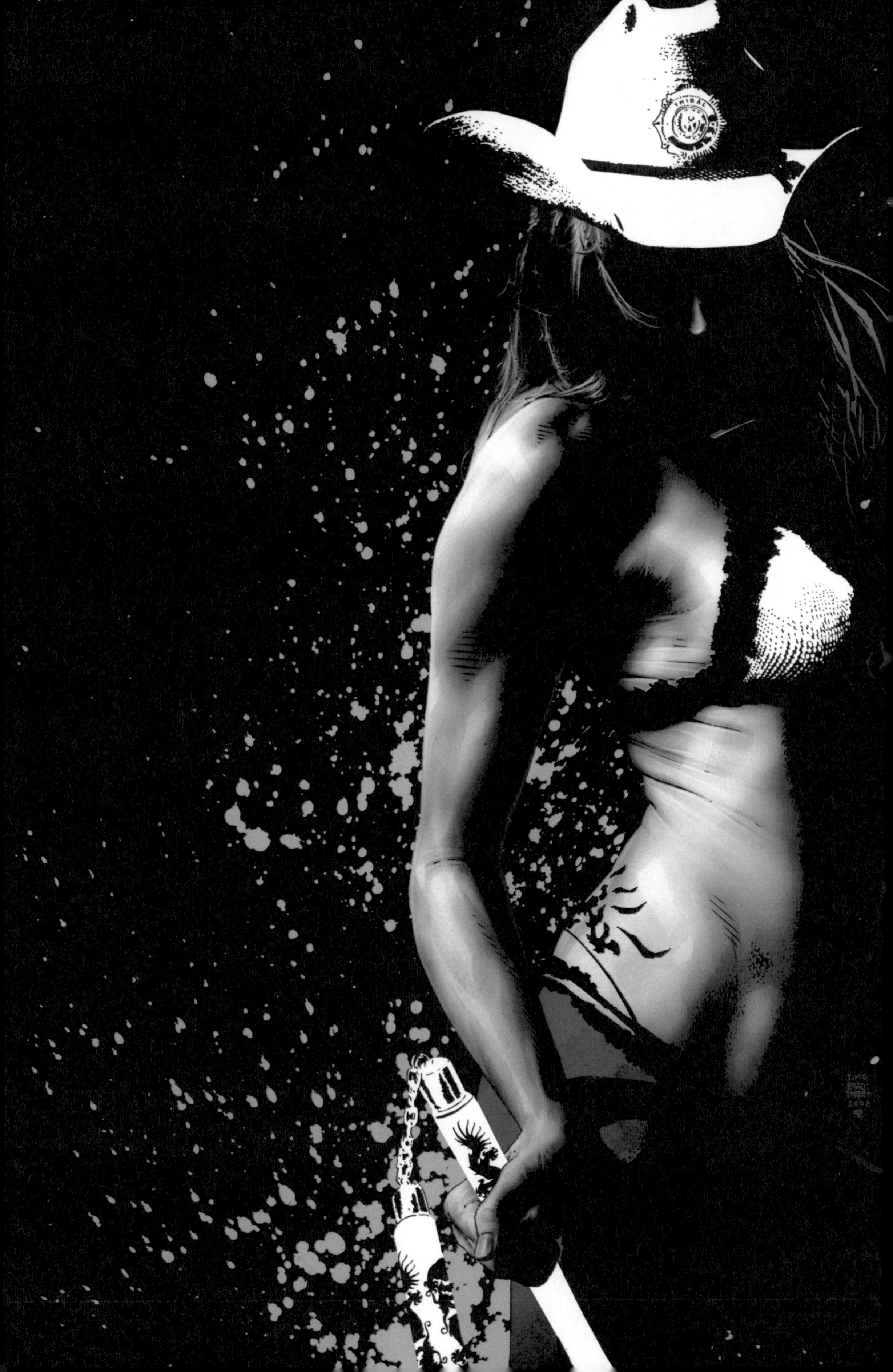

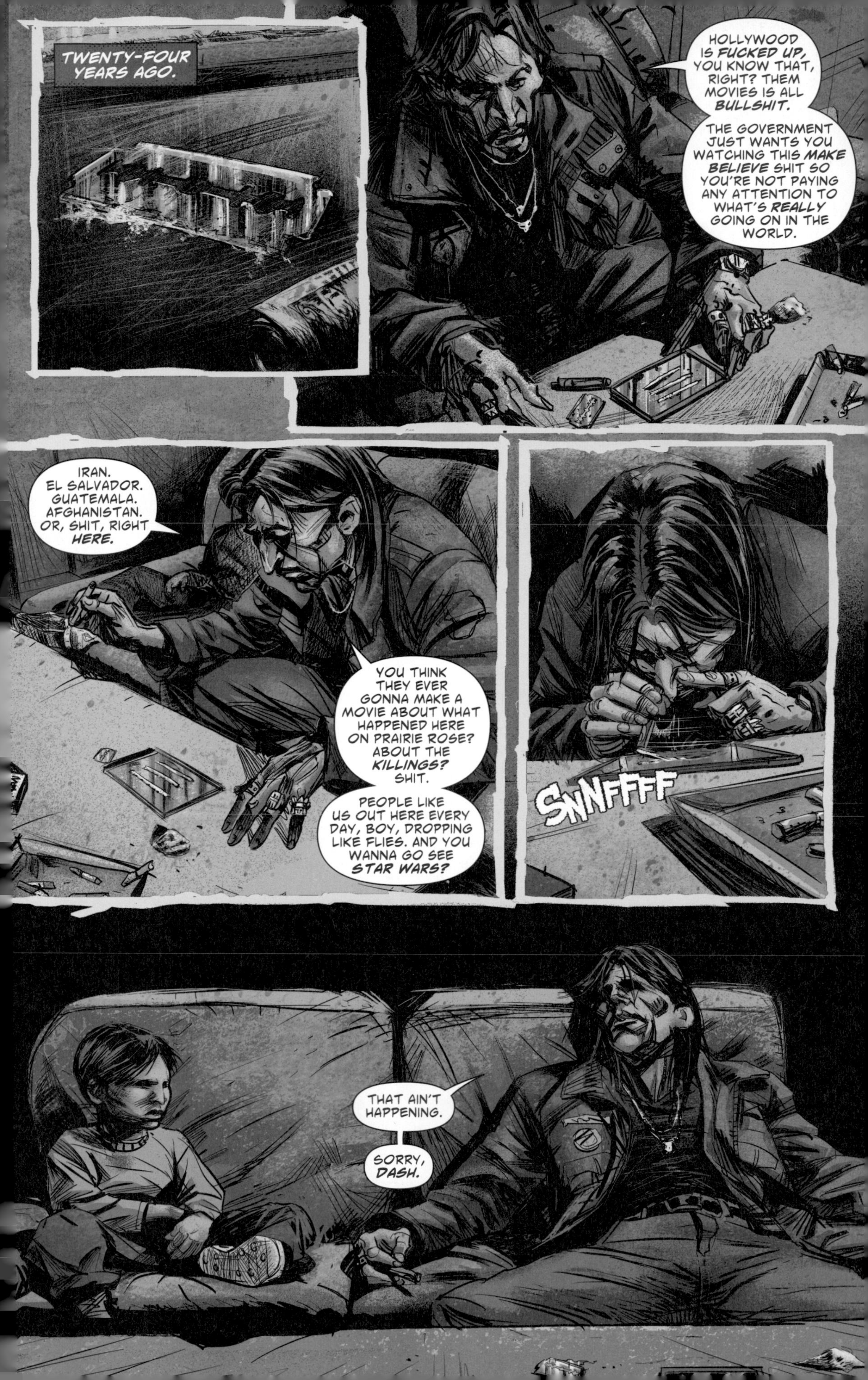
TWENTY-FOUR YEARS AGO.
HOLLYWOOD IS **FUCKED UP,** YOU KNOW THAT, RIGHT? THEM MOVIES IS ALL **BULLSHIT.**
THE GOVERNMENT JUST WANTS YOU WATCHING THIS **MAKE BELIEVE** SHIT SO YOU'RE NOT PAYING ANY ATTENTION TO WHAT'S **REALLY** GOING ON IN THE WORLD.
IRAN. EL SALVADOR. GUATEMALA. AFGHANISTAN. OR, SHIT, RIGHT **HERE.**
YOU THINK THEY EVER GONNA MAKE A MOVIE ABOUT WHAT HAPPENED HERE ON PRAIRIE ROSE? ABOUT THE **KILLINGS?** SHIT.
PEOPLE LIKE US OUT HERE EVERY DAY, BOY, DROPPING LIKE FLIES. AND YOU WANNA GO SEE **STAR WARS?**
SNNFFFF
THAT AIN'T HAPPENING.
SORRY, **DASH.**

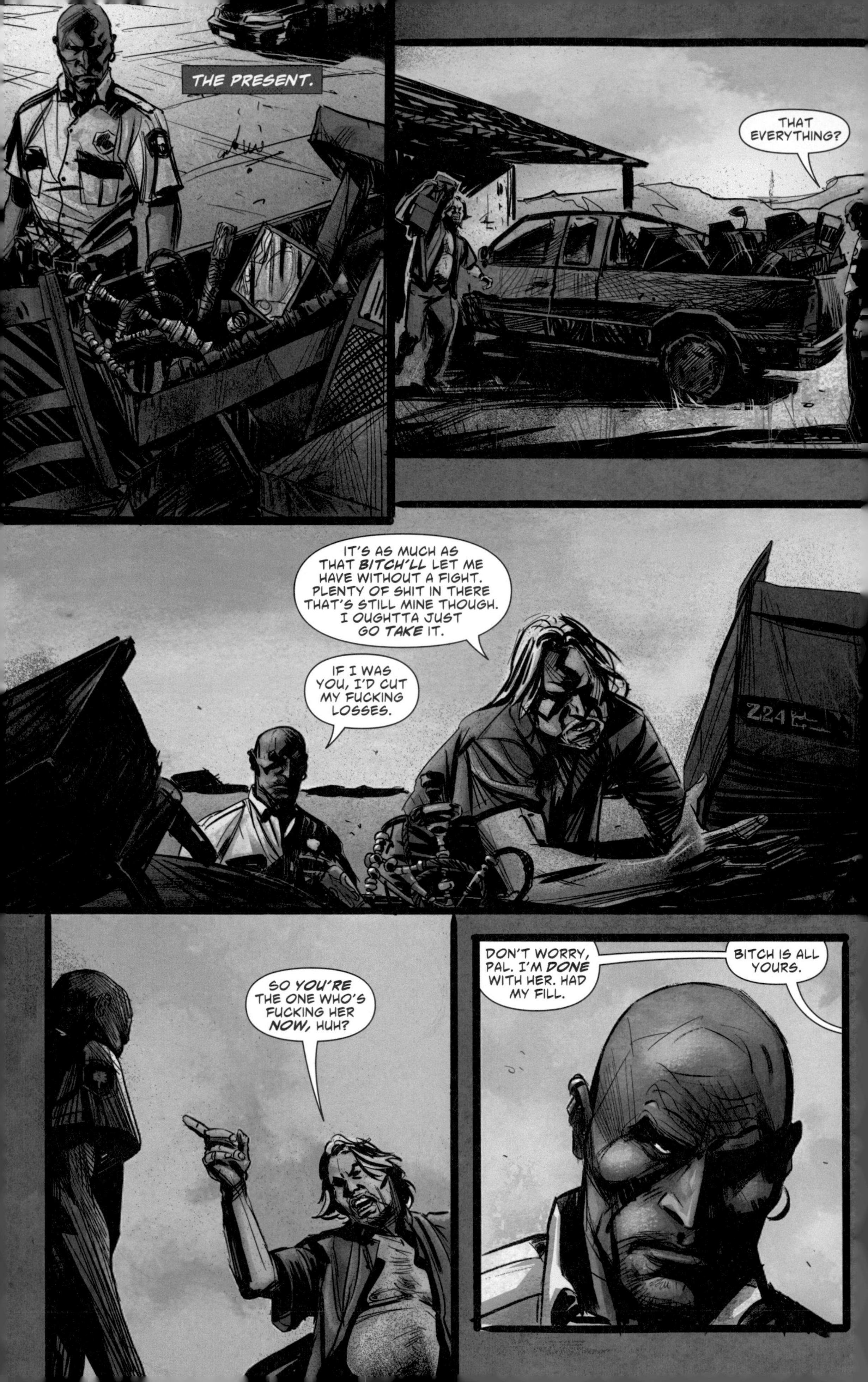
THE PRESENT.
THAT EVERYTHING?
IT'S AS MUCH AS THAT BITCH'LL LET ME HAVE WITHOUT A FIGHT. PLENTY OF SHIT IN THERE THAT'S STILL MINE THOUGH. I OUGHTTA JUST GO TAKE IT.
IF I WAS YOU, I'D CUT MY FUCKING LOSSES.
Z24
SO YOU'RE THE ONE WHO'S FUCKING HER NOW, HUH?
DON'T WORRY, PAL. I'M DONE WITH HER. HAD MY FILL.
BITCH IS ALL YOURS.

HEH.

GOOD LUCK.

HA HA HAA HAAA

SWEET DREAMS, PRINCESS.

JUST GIVE IT HERE, ASSHOLE.

SEVEN YEARS AGO.

GRAHAM?

IT'S ME, BABY. C'MON, IT'S TIME TO GO. WE GOTTA LEAVE *NOW*.

NOW? BUT I'M NOT EVEN PACKED, I DON'T--

NO TIME, BABY. WE'LL WORRY ABOUT THAT LATER.

OH MY GOD, GRAHAM, WHAT HAPPENED TO YOUR CAR? ARE THOSE *BULLET HOLES?*

JUST GET IN THE CAR, CAROL. I'LL EXPLAIN EVERYTHING AS WE GO.

GRAHAM... HOLY SHIT, IS THAT...

YEAH.

IT'S OUR TICKET *OUT* OF HERE.

THE BOUDOIR STOMP PART TWO

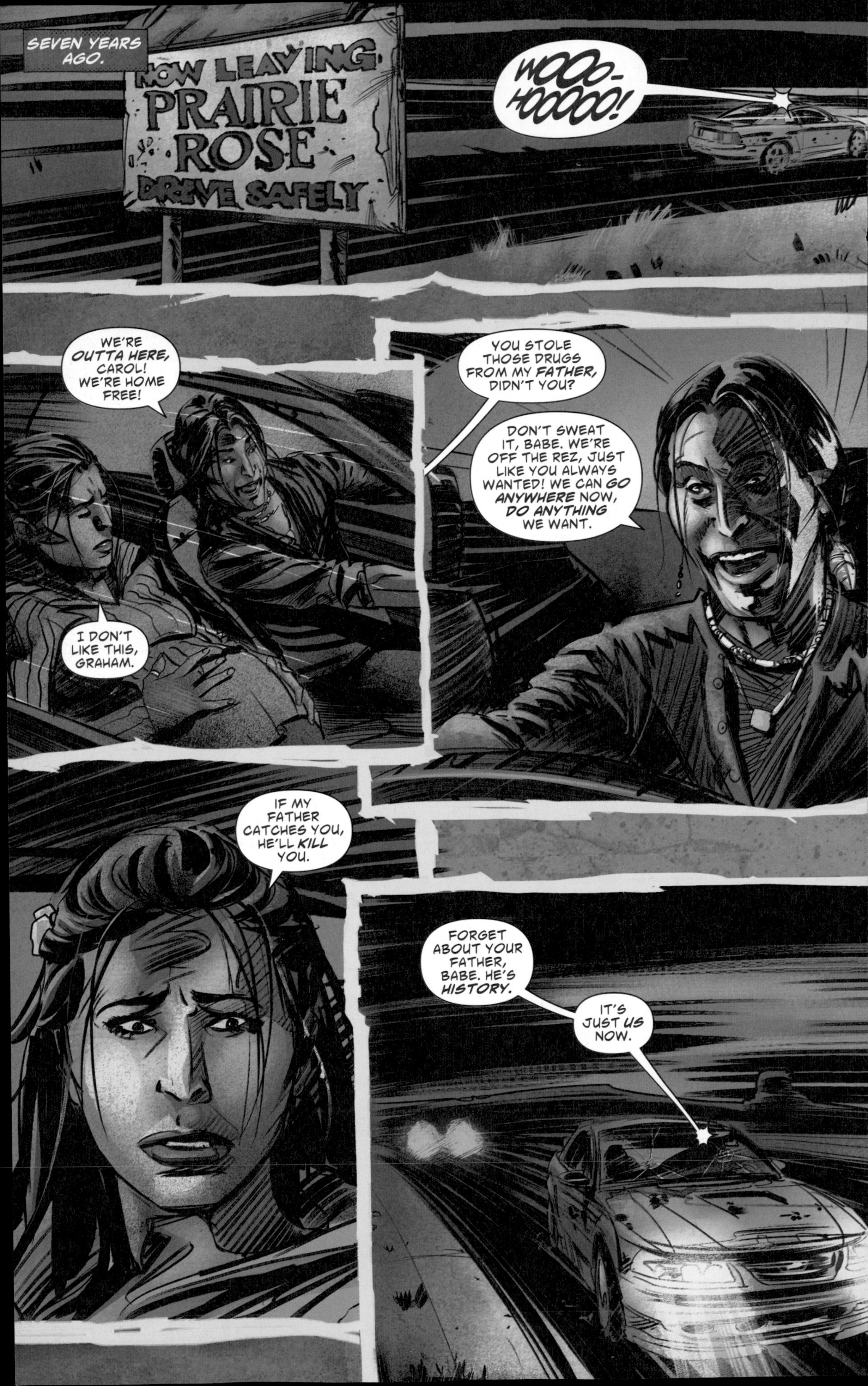
SEVEN YEARS AGO.
NOW LEAVING PRAIRIE ROSE
DRIVE SAFELY
WOOO-HOOOOO!
WE'RE OUTTA HERE, CAROL! WE'RE HOME FREE!
I DON'T LIKE THIS, GRAHAM.
YOU STOLE THOSE DRUGS FROM MY FATHER, DIDN'T YOU?
DON'T SWEAT IT, BABE. WE'RE OFF THE REZ, JUST LIKE YOU ALWAYS WANTED! WE CAN GO ANYWHERE NOW, DO ANYTHING WE WANT.
IF MY FATHER CATCHES YOU, HE'LL KILL YOU.
FORGET ABOUT YOUR FATHER, BABE. HE'S HISTORY.
IT'S JUST US NOW.

'NOTHER SNORT, BAD HORSE?

WHAT DO YOU THINK?

I THINK ONE OF THESE NIGHTS, MY FRIEND...

...YOU'RE GONNA DRINK YOUR DUMB ASS TO DEATH.

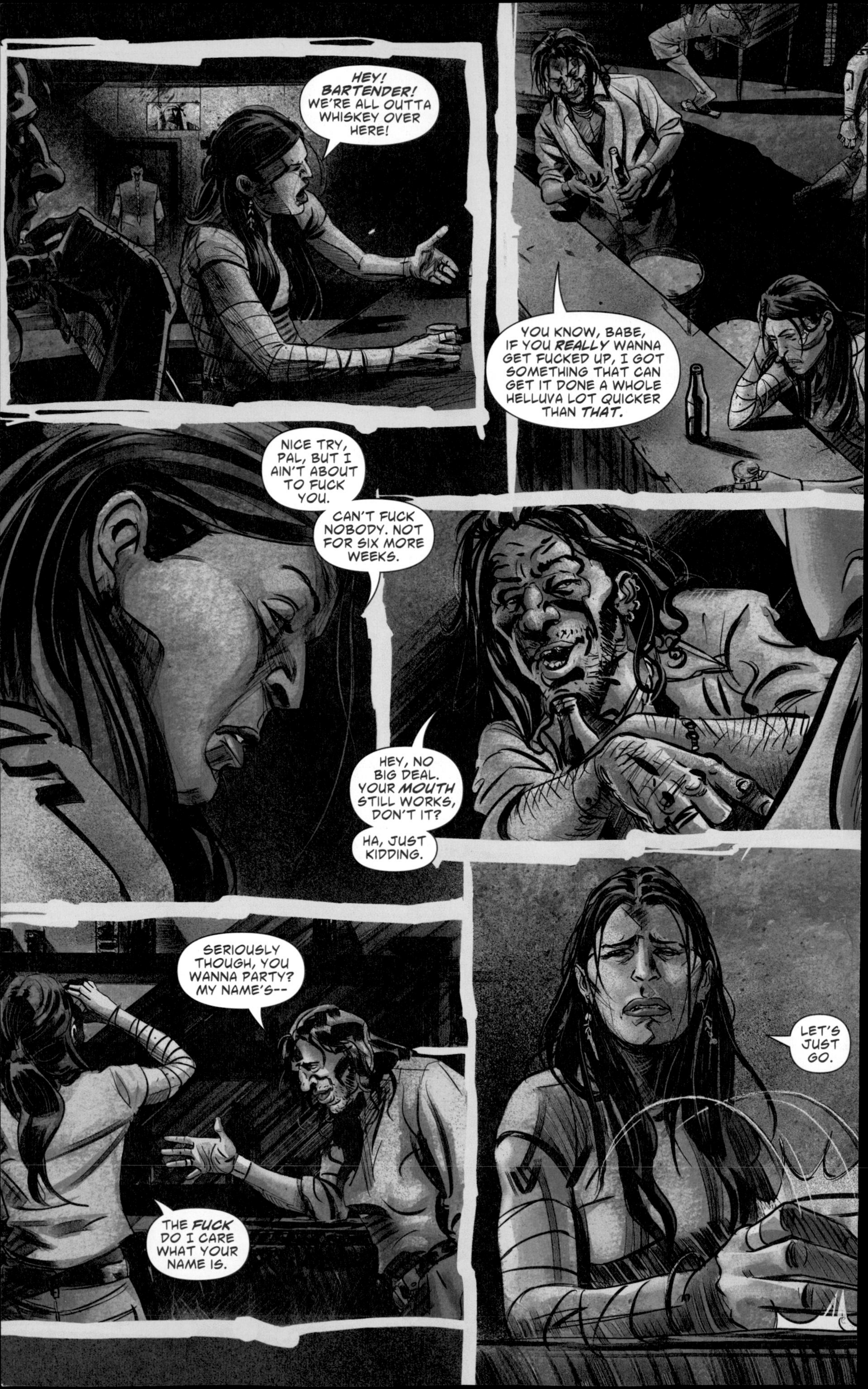
HEY! BARTENDER! WE'RE ALL OUTTA WHISKEY OVER HERE!
YOU KNOW, BABE, IF YOU REALLY WANNA GET FUCKED UP, I GOT SOMETHING THAT CAN GET IT DONE A WHOLE HELLUVA LOT QUICKER THAN THAT.
NICE TRY, PAL, BUT I AIN'T ABOUT TO FUCK YOU.
CAN'T FUCK NOBODY. NOT FOR SIX MORE WEEKS.
HEY, NO BIG DEAL. YOUR MOUTH STILL WORKS, DON'T IT?
HA, JUST KIDDING.
SERIOUSLY THOUGH, YOU WANNA PARTY? MY NAME'S--
THE FUCK DO I CARE WHAT YOUR NAME IS.
LET'S JUST GO.

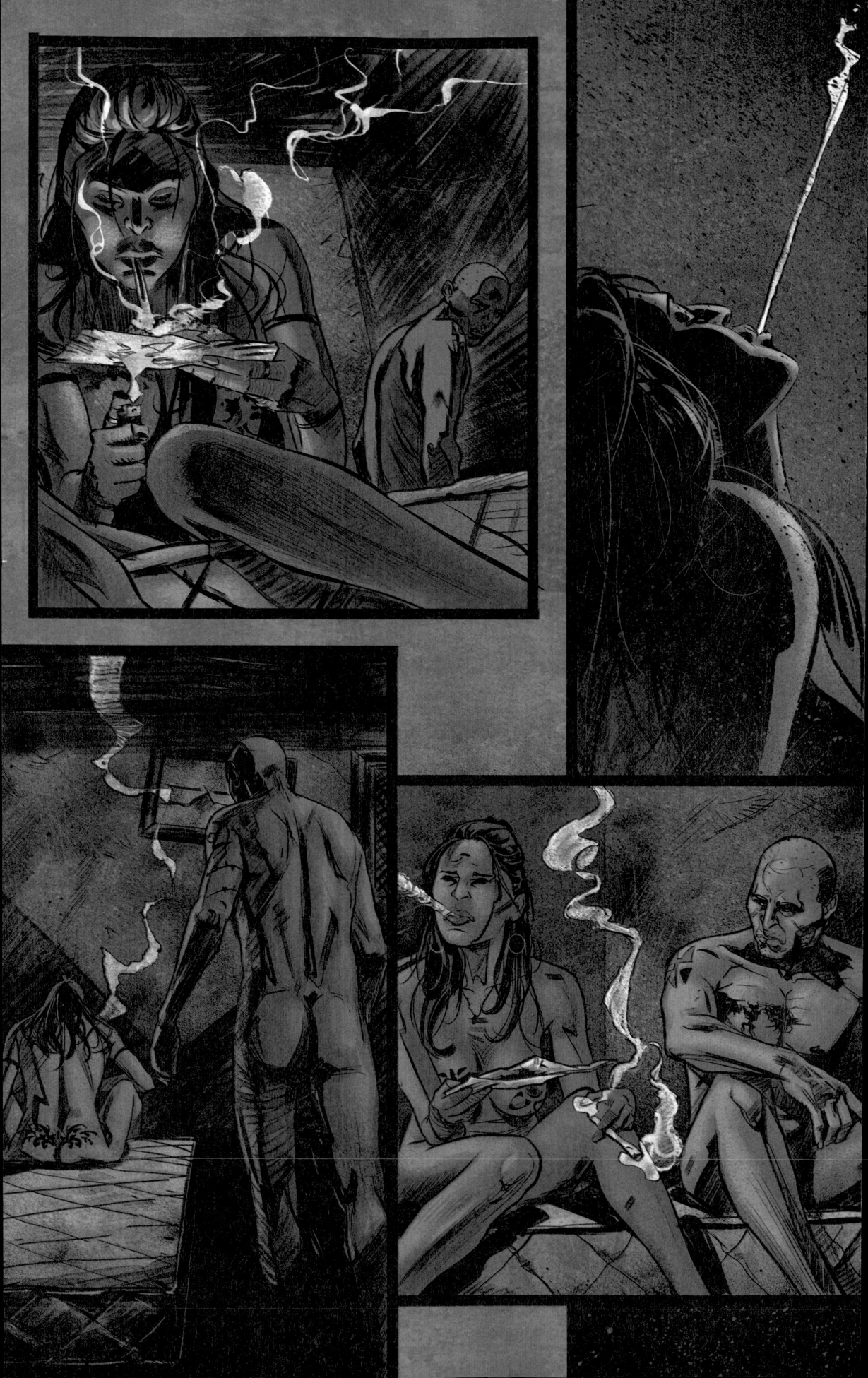

YOU FIND OUT WHAT I ASKED?

NOT YET. BUT I'M KEEPING THE BODIES UNDER WRAPS, HOPING I'LL GET LUCKY WITH A MISSING PERSONS REPORT.

I STILL THINK THIS IS A *BAD* IDEA THOUGH. WE SHOULD JUST DISAPPEAR THESE KIDS AND LET--

I KNOW WHAT YOU THINK. AND YOU KNOW WHAT I TOLD YOU TO DO, SO DO IT.

I WANNA KNOW WHO THEY WERE.

BOSS.

SOMEBODY'S ASKING TO SEE YA. SOME OLD WOMAN. SAYS IT'S IMPORTANT.

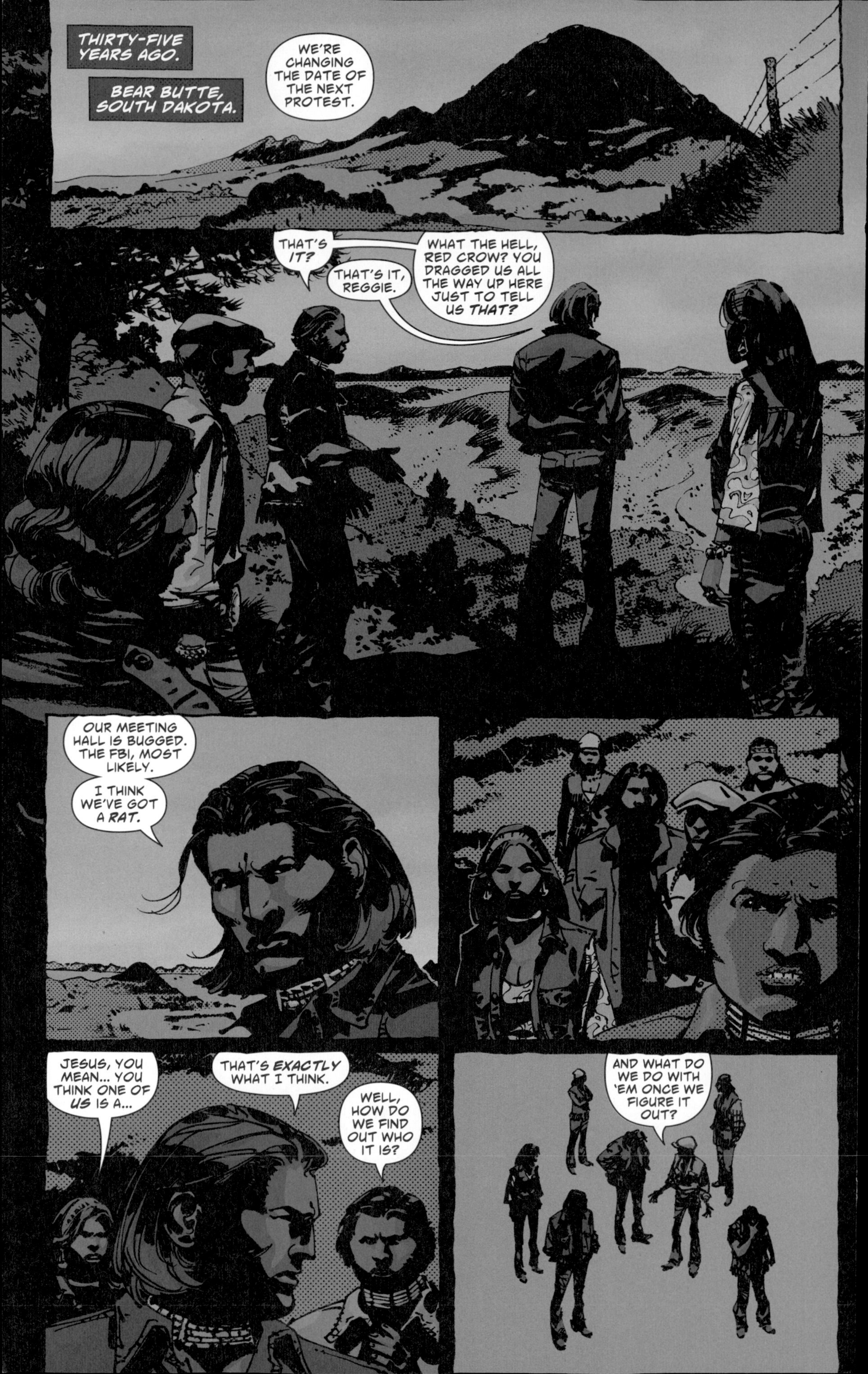
THIRTY-FIVE YEARS AGO.
BEAR BUTTE, SOUTH DAKOTA.
WE'RE CHANGING THE DATE OF THE NEXT PROTEST.
THAT'S IT?
WHAT THE HELL, RED CROW? YOU DRAGGED US ALL THE WAY UP HERE JUST TO TELL US THAT?
THAT'S IT, REGGIE.
OUR MEETING HALL IS BUGGED. THE FBI, MOST LIKELY.
I THINK WE'VE GOT A RAT.
JESUS, YOU MEAN... YOU THINK ONE OF US IS A...
THAT'S EXACTLY WHAT I THINK.
WELL, HOW DO WE FIND OUT WHO IT IS?
AND WHAT DO WE DO WITH 'EM ONCE WE FIGURE IT OUT?

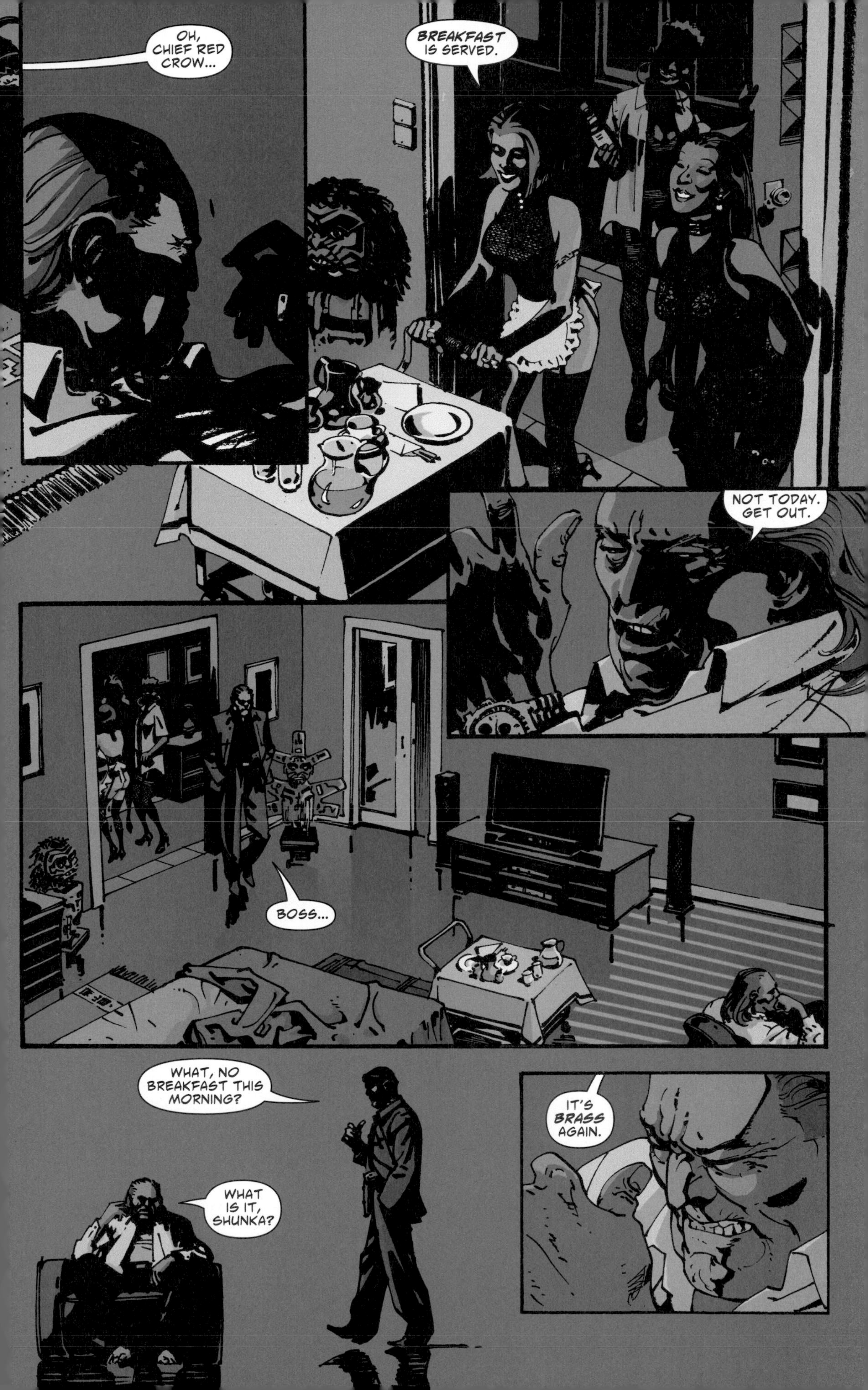
OH, CHIEF RED CROW...
BREAKFAST IS SERVED.
NOT TODAY. GET OUT.
BOSS...
WHAT, NO BREAKFAST THIS MORNING?
WHAT IS IT, SHUNKA?
IT'S BRASS AGAIN.

LISTEN, I KNOW SOME BOYS IN MINNESOTA. I CAN MAKE SOME INQUIRIES, SEE WHAT IT'D COST TO--

NO. I DON'T WANT A FUCKING *WAR.*

YOU TELL OUR BOYS TO TIGHTEN UP. NO EXTRACURRICULAR ACTIVITIES FOR A WHILE. LET BRASS THINK HE'S MADE HIS POINT.

AND TELL TIM'S PEOPLE THAT BRASS IS *NOT* TO BE TOUCHED. TELL 'EM I'LL MAKE RIGHT WHAT HE DONE.

I'M TELLING YOU, HE AIN'T GONNA STOP. HE'LL FIND AN EXCUSE.

ANYTHING ELSE YOU GOT TO TELL ME?!

YEAH.

THOSE TWO *KIDS* BRASS KILLED THE OTHER DAY. YOU SAID YOU WANTED TO KNOW WHO THEY WERE...

ONE'S A RUNAWAY FROM THE RED SAGE REZ. NO FAMILY. NOBODY EVEN LOOKING FOR HIM.

OTHER'S A GIRL FROM HERE IN TOWN. *GERALDINE STANDING ROCK.* METH ADDICT. WHORE.

STANDING ROCK?

YEAH. YOU KNOW HER?

"I KNEW HER *GRANDFATHER*."

BEEN *WHAT?* THIRTY-FIVE YEARS NOW SINCE REGGIE DISAPPEARED?

SOMETIMES IT'S HARD TO REMEMBER HE EVER EXISTED.

I'M SORRY, *PHYLLIS.* I DIDN'T COME BY TO DREDGE UP OLD MEMORIES.

I CAME BECAUSE I HEARD ABOUT YOUR *GRANDDAUGHTER.* THAT SHE WAS *MISSING.*

GERALDINE. THAT POOR GIRL AIN'T NEVER HAD A CHANCE. BEEN IN TROUBLE EVER SINCE SHE WAS OLD ENOUGH TO KNOW BETTER.

HEY, RED CROW.

WHERE'S EVERYBODY ELSE AT? I THOUGHT WE WERE HAVING A MEETING.

RED CROW?

I HOPE YOU AT LEAST *STRUGGLED* WITH THE DECISION TO SELL US OUT, REGGIE. I'D HATE TO THINK IT CAME EASY.

WHAT? LINCOLN, WHAT IS THIS?

WHAT'D THEY OFFER YOU? TELL ME IT WAS SOMETHING OTHER THAN JUST MONEY. PLEASE TELL ME YOU HAD SOMETHING *ELSE* TO GAIN.

LOOK, I DON'T KNOW WHAT--

FIRST THING YOU LEARN WHEN YOU WITNESS A *KILLING* IS IT AIN'T AT ALL LIKE IT IS IN THE *MOVIES*.

IN THE WESTERNS I WATCHED AS A KID, A 'COWBOY'D TAKE AN ARROW IN THE BACK AND INSTANTLY FALL OVER DEAD.

FIRST MAN I EVER KILLED...

...I HAD TO STRANGLE FOR 11 MINUTES.

THERE'S NEVER ANY GLORY OR HONOR IN SOMETHING LIKE THAT.

THERE'S JUST THE *HOWLS*.

THE GUTTURAL SORT OF SOUNDS YOU DON'T NEVER HEAR A BODY MAKE EXCEPT WHEN IT'S DYING.

USUALLY THEY'LL SHIT THEIR PANTS. SOMETIMES YOU WILL TOO.

SOMETIMES AFTERWARDS YOU'LL PASS OUT FROM EXHAUSTION. OTHER TIMES YOU'LL BE SO JACKED UP ON ADRENALINE THAT YOU COULD RUN A GODDAMN MARATHON.

IN THE END YOU'LL FIND YOURSELF STANDING OVER SOMETHING THAT DON'T EVEN SEEM *HUMAN* NO MORE.

AND YOU'LL SWEAR TO YOURSELF THAT YOU WON'T *NEVER* DO THIS AGAIN, SO LONG AS YOU LIVE.

AND SOMETIMES YOU MIGHT EVEN BELIEVE THE *LIE*.

PPWHBLYAAC!

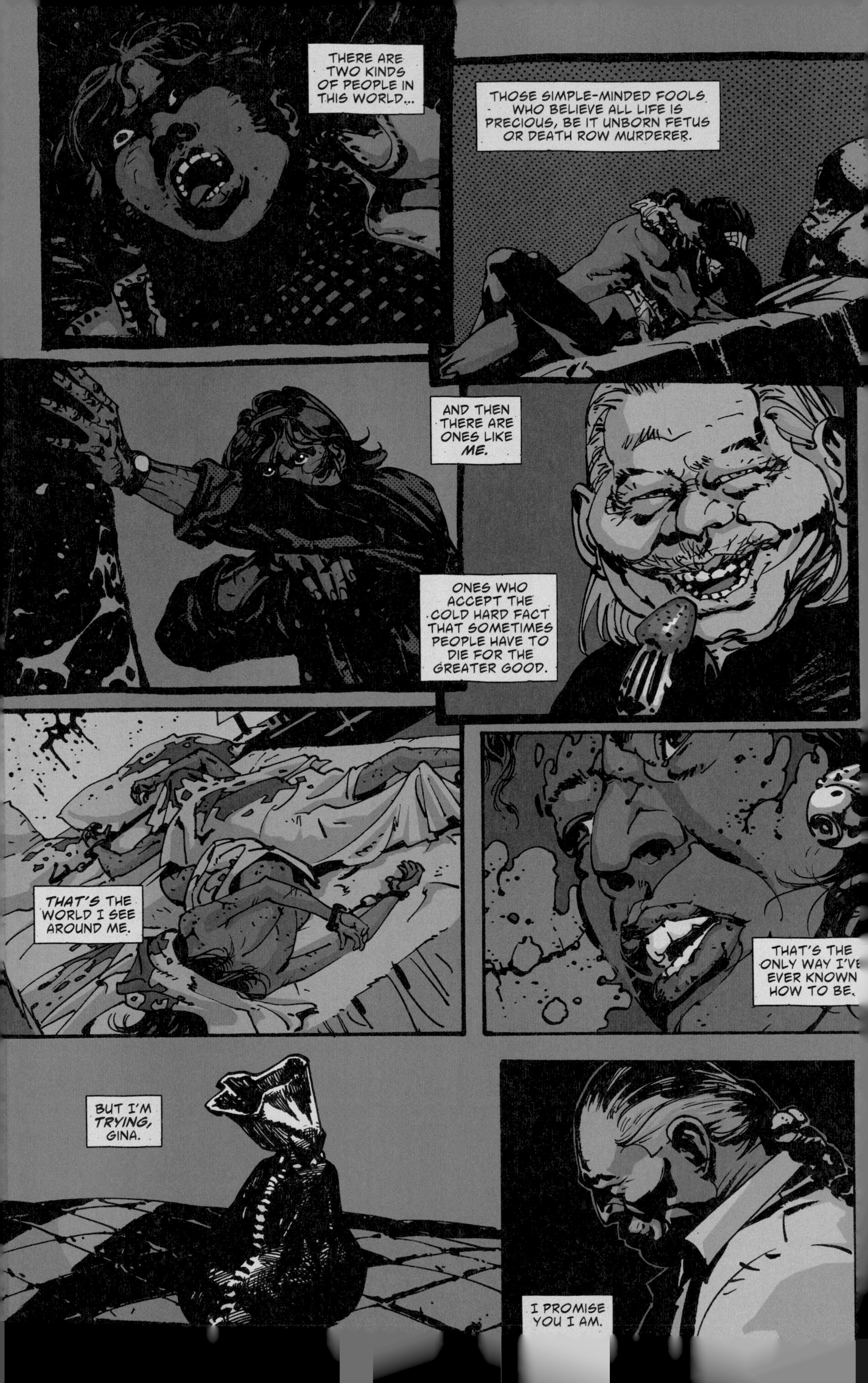
THERE ARE TWO KINDS OF PEOPLE IN THIS WORLD...
THOSE SIMPLE-MINDED FOOLS WHO BELIEVE ALL LIFE IS PRECIOUS, BE IT UNBORN FETUS OR DEATH ROW MURDERER.
AND THEN THERE ARE ONES LIKE *ME*.
ONES WHO ACCEPT THE COLD HARD FACT THAT SOMETIMES PEOPLE HAVE TO DIE FOR THE GREATER GOOD.
THAT'S THE WORLD I SEE AROUND ME.
THAT'S THE ONLY WAY I'VE EVER KNOWN HOW TO BE.
BUT I'M *TRYING*, GINA.
I PROMISE YOU I AM.

WHERE DID YOU *GET* THIS?

WHAT? FROM WORK.

THEY DON'T PAY YOU THIS WELL TO MOP FLOORS. WHERE DID YOU GET THIS?

GRANNY...

BEFORE YOU ANSWER, YOU JUST REMEMBER WHAT I TOLD YOU THE *LAST* TIME YOU GOT INTO TROUBLE WITH THE LAW.

I TOLD YOU IF IT HAPPENED AGAIN, I'D KICK YOU OUT OF MY HOUSE FOR GOOD, YOU REMEMBER THAT?

YEAH, BUT--

I *MEANT* IT TOO.

GRANNY, C'MON, CALM DOWN, THERE'S NOTHING TO WORRY ABOUT.

I FIND OUT YOU'RE SELLING DRUGS, I'LL CALL THE POLICE ON YOU MYSELF, YOU HEAR?

GRANNY, DON'T WORRY, OKAY?

I *WORK* FOR THE POLICE NOW.

WHEN I WAS IN SECOND GRADE, A MAN CAME TO SPEAK TO OUR CLASS.

AN *ASTRONAUT*.

HE TALKED ABOUT WALKING ON THE MOON. ABOUT HOW BEAUTIFUL THE VIEW WAS FROM UP THERE.

I BECAME OBSESSED WITH BEING JUST LIKE HIM.

I DRANK MY TANG, ATE MY WHEATIES AND DREAMED EVERY NIGHT ABOUT FLYING THROUGH SPACE.

IT'S KINDA FUNNY WHEN YOU THINK ABOUT IT NOW...

ME DREAMING ABOUT LEAVING THE EARTH AND GOING ALL THE WAY TO THE MOON...

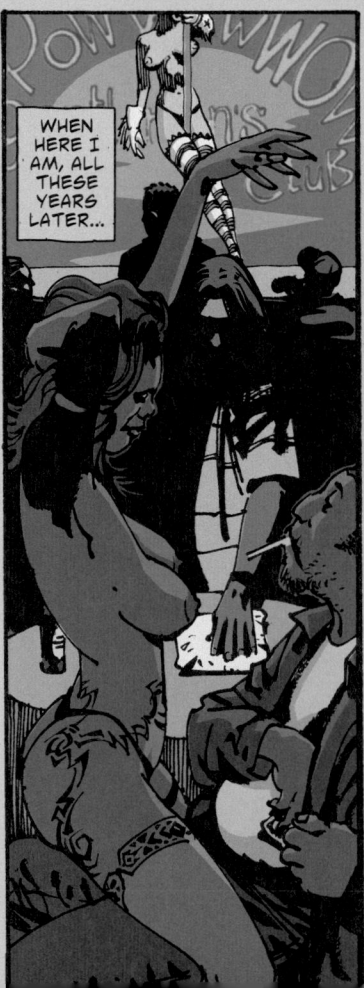

WHEN HERE I AM, ALL THESE YEARS LATER...

AND I CAN'T EVEN GET THE FUCK OUT OF SHANNON COUNTY, SOUTH DAKOTA.

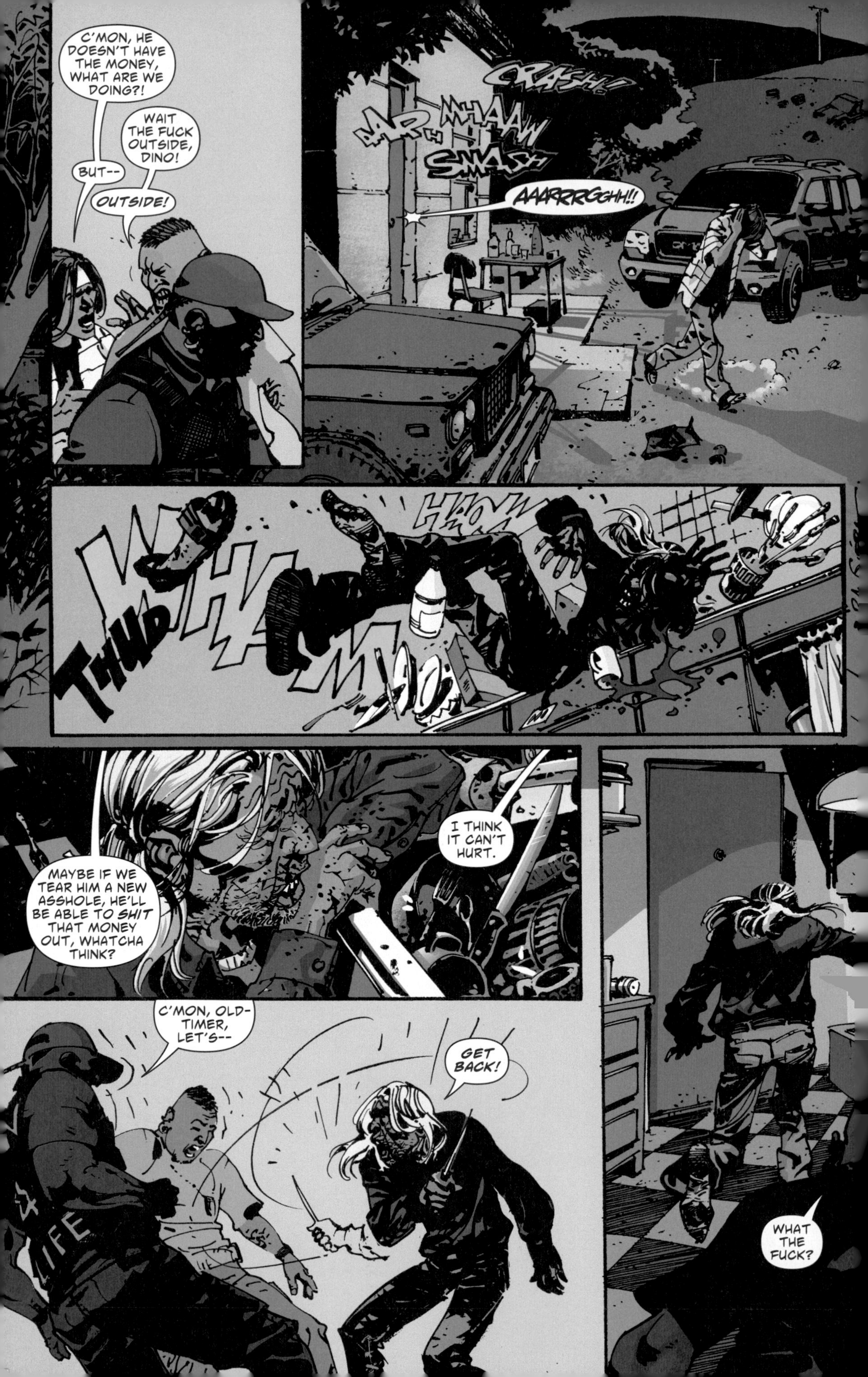
C'MON, HE DOESN'T HAVE THE MONEY, WHAT ARE WE DOING?!
WAIT THE FUCK OUTSIDE, DINO!
BUT--
OUTSIDE!
CRASH!
AARH
WHAAAW
SMASH
AAARRRGGHH!!
THUD
WHAM
MAYBE IF WE TEAR HIM A NEW ASSHOLE, HE'LL BE ABLE TO SHIT THAT MONEY OUT, WHATCHA THINK?
I THINK IT CAN'T HURT.
C'MON, OLD-TIMER, LET'S--
GET BACK!
WHAT THE FUCK?

OW

THUP

GRANNY, C'MON, I'M TIRED. LET'S NOT DO THIS RIGHT NOW.

YOUR SISTER'S IN THE HOSPITAL.

WHAT'S THIS?

YOUR THINGS. YOU DON'T LIVE HERE ANYMORE.

SHE WAS PASSED OUT IN THE BACKYARD FROM SMOKING GOD KNOWS WHAT KINDA MESS. SHE MAY LOSE THE BABY.

GRANNY--

YOU BROUGHT THAT JUNK INTO MY HOUSE, DINO. I CAN'T HAVE YOU HERE NO MORE.

KRYSTAL'S AN ADDICT, GRANNY. SHE'S ALWAYS BEEN AN ADDICT. THAT AIN'T MY FUCKING FAULT.

YOU AIN'T COMING IN HERE. I'LL CALL THE POLICE IF I HAVE TO.

THE GRAVEL IN YOUR GUTS PART FOUR

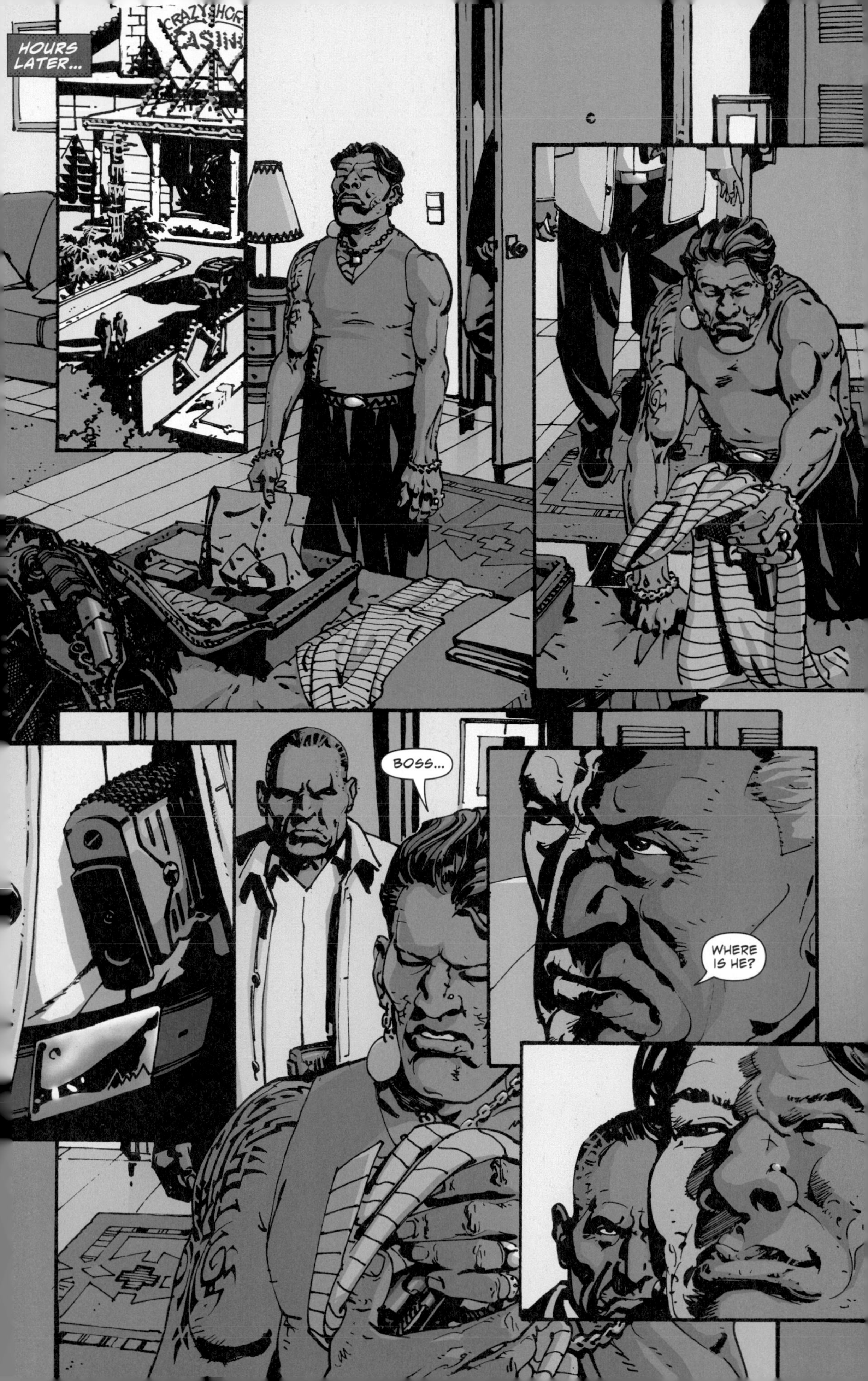
HOURS LATER...
CRAZYSHOR
CASIN
BOSS...
WHERE IS HE?

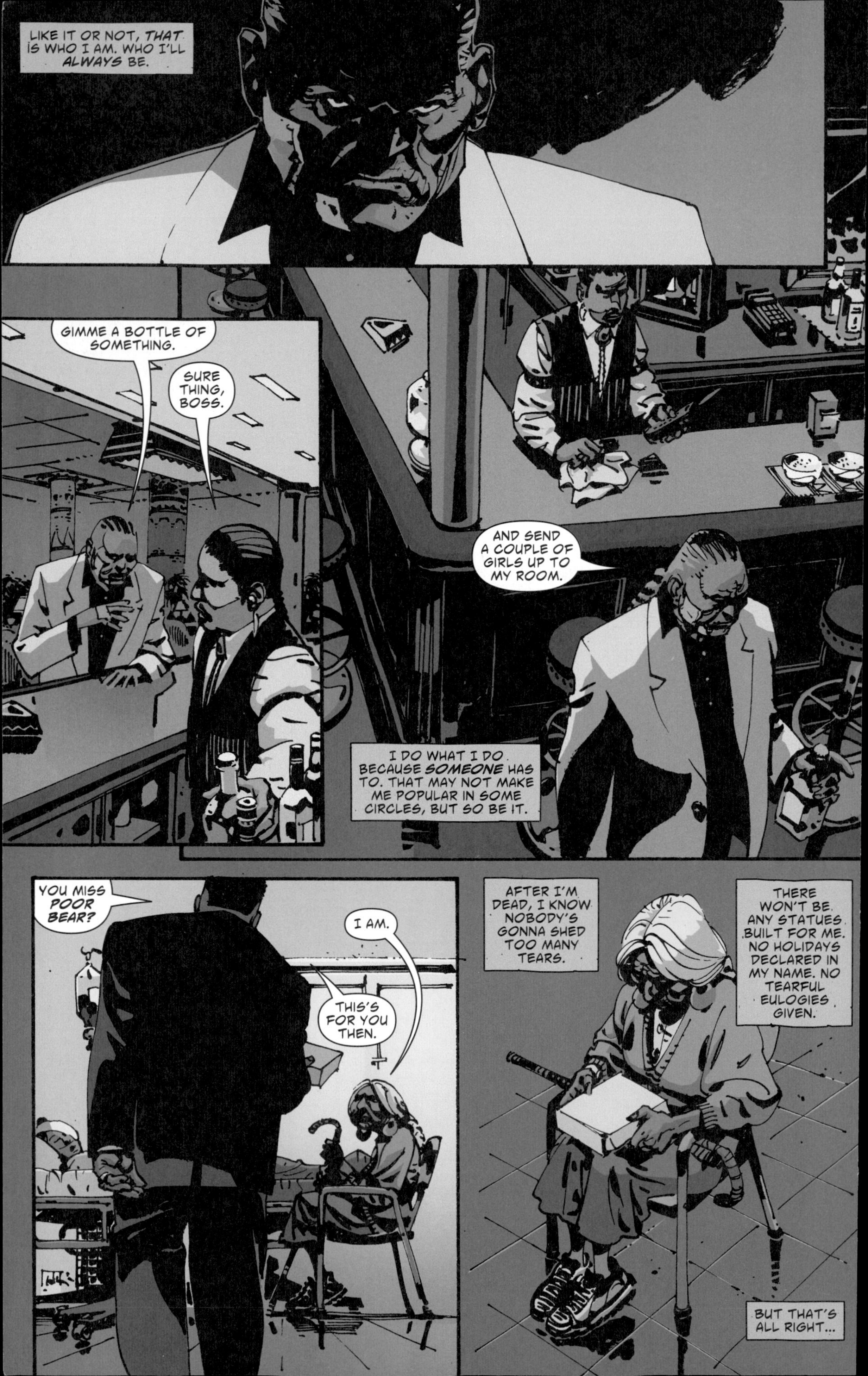
LIKE IT OR NOT, *THAT* IS WHO I AM. WHO I'LL *ALWAYS* BE.
GIMME A BOTTLE OF SOMETHING.
SURE THING, BOSS.
AND SEND A COUPLE OF GIRLS UP TO MY ROOM.
I DO WHAT I DO. BECAUSE *SOMEONE* HAS TO. THAT MAY NOT MAKE ME POPULAR IN SOME CIRCLES, BUT SO BE IT.
YOU MISS *POOR BEAR?*
I AM.
THIS'S FOR YOU THEN.
AFTER I'M DEAD, I KNOW NOBODY'S GONNA SHED TOO MANY TEARS.
THERE WON'T BE ANY STATUES BUILT FOR ME. NO HOLIDAYS DECLARED IN MY NAME. NO TEARFUL EULOGIES GIVEN.
BUT THAT'S ALL RIGHT...

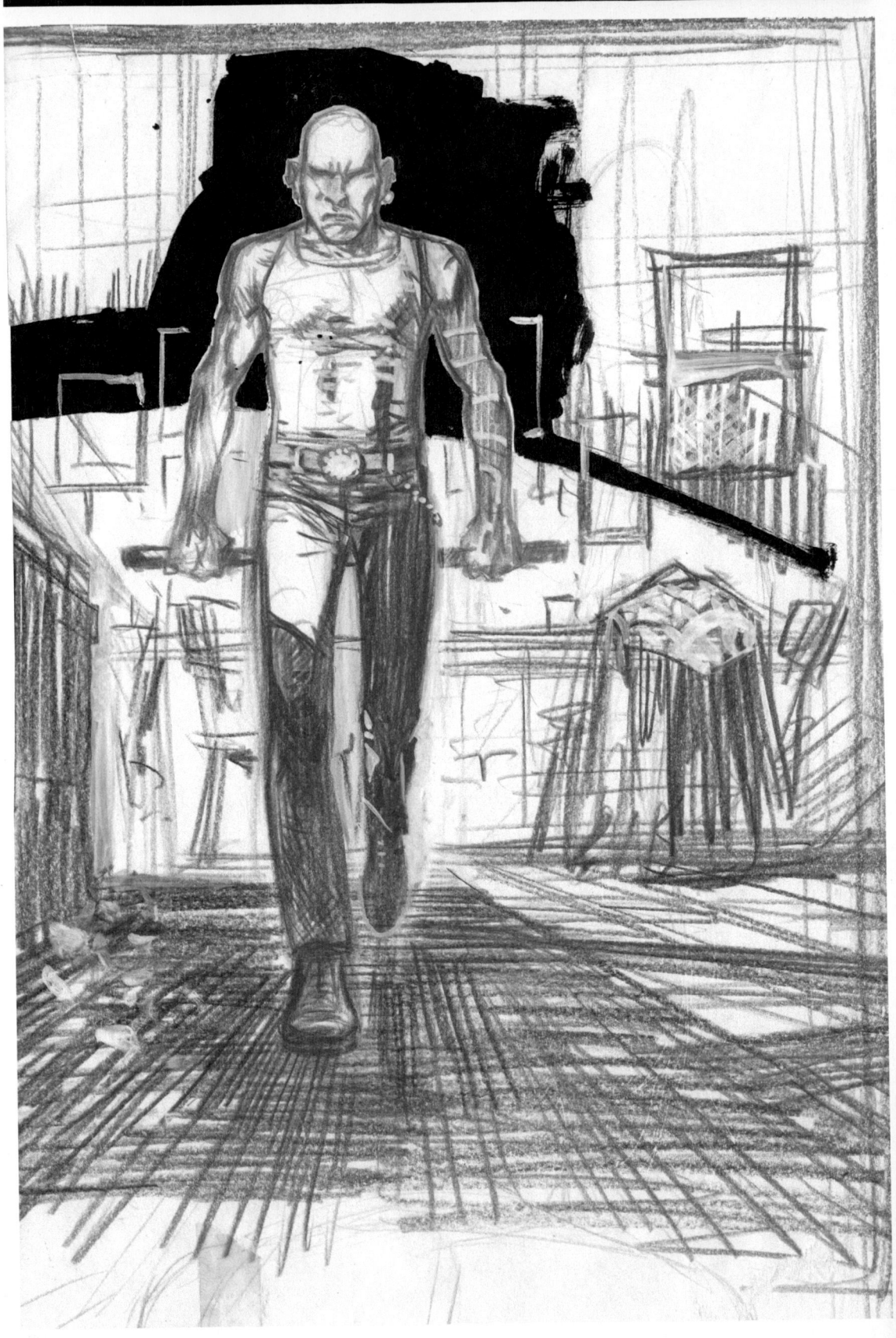

MR. BRASS.

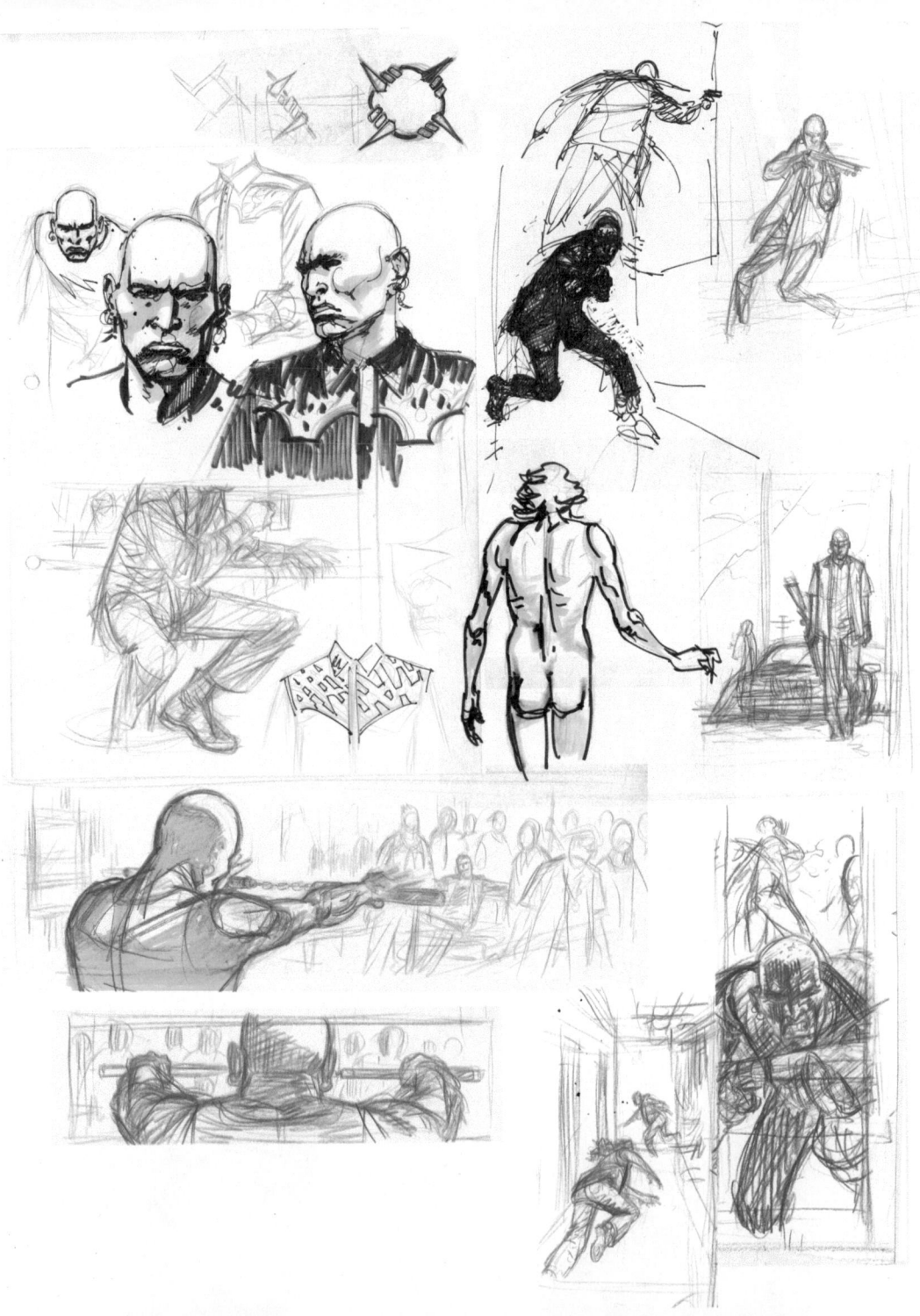

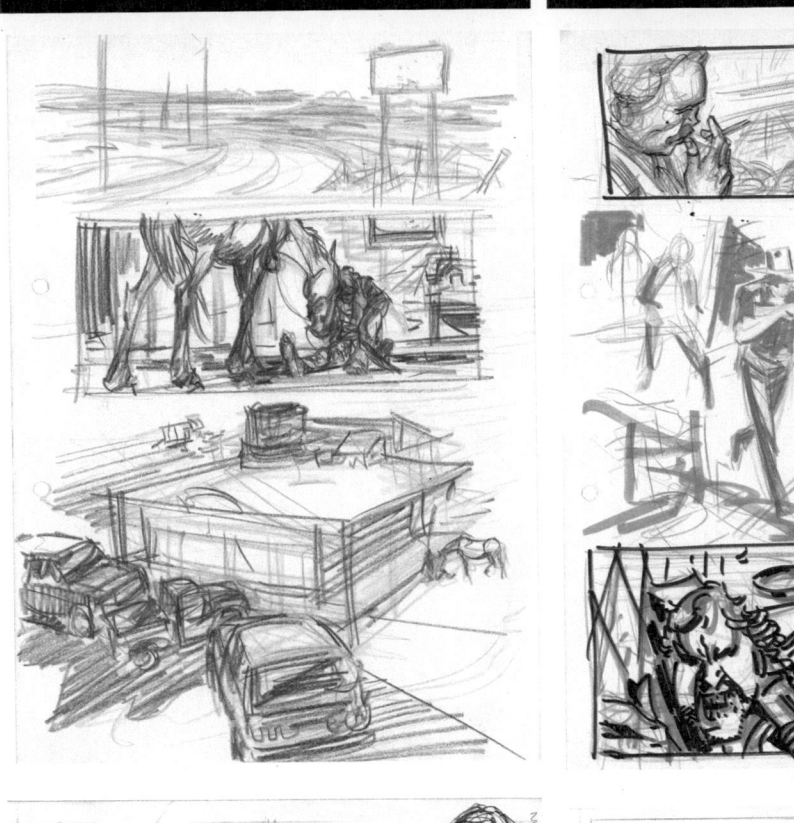

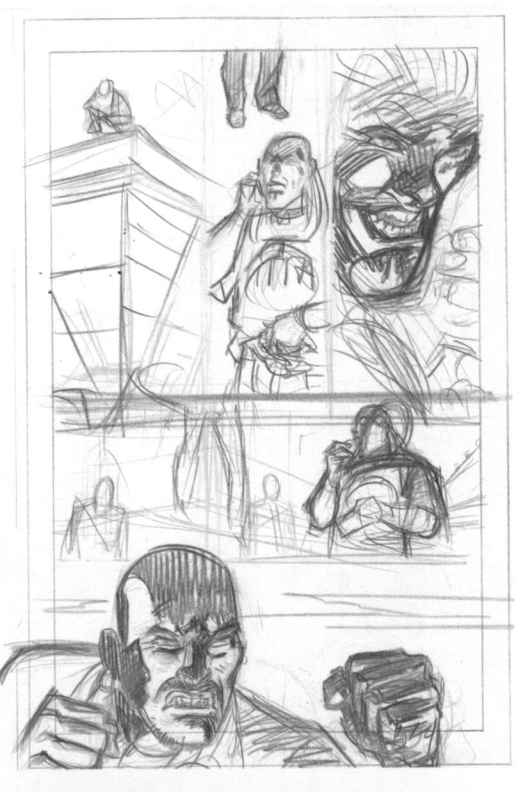

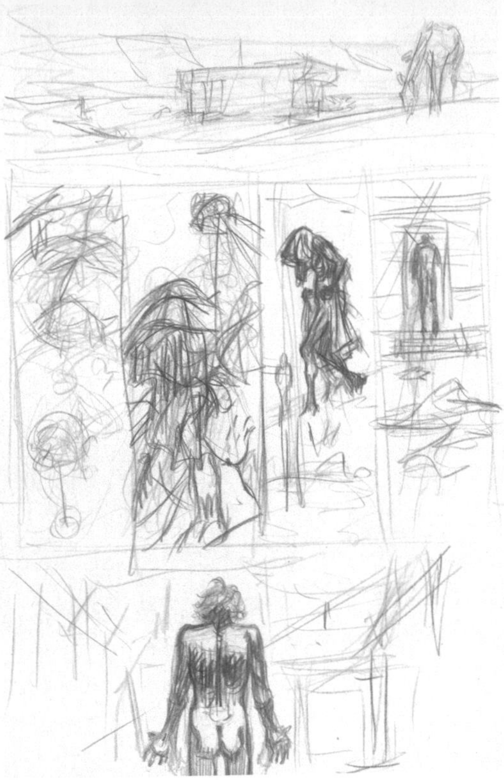

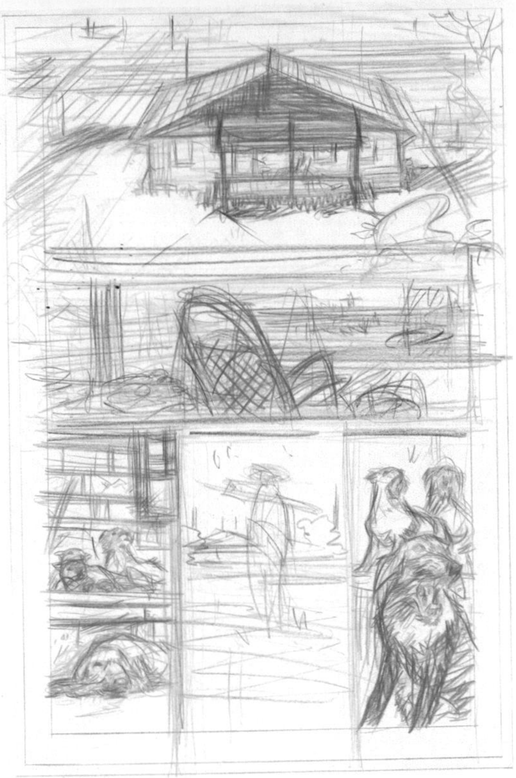

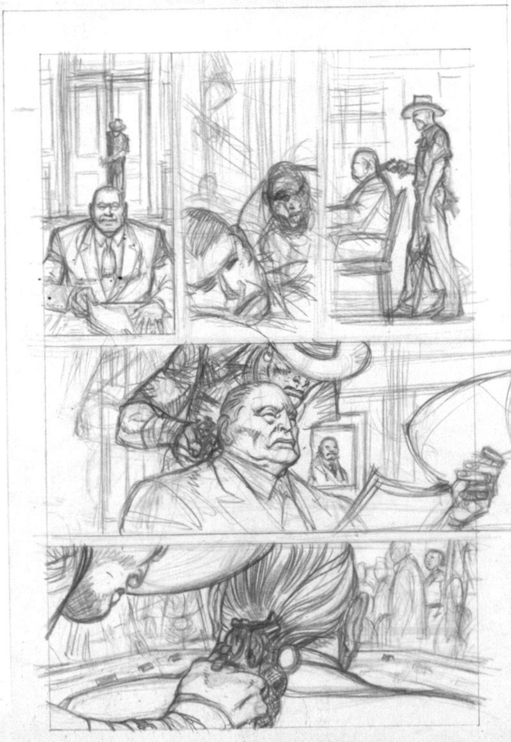

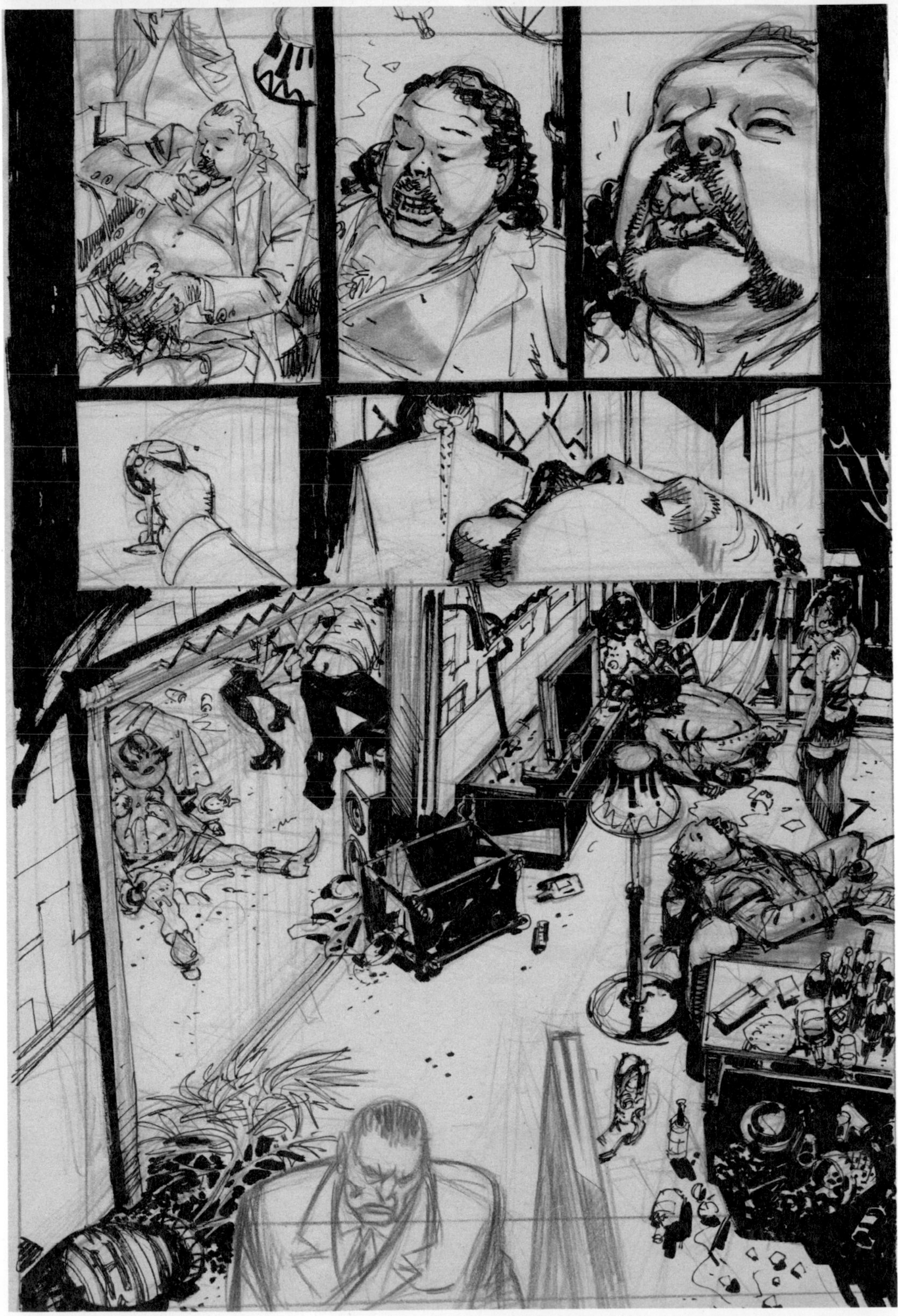

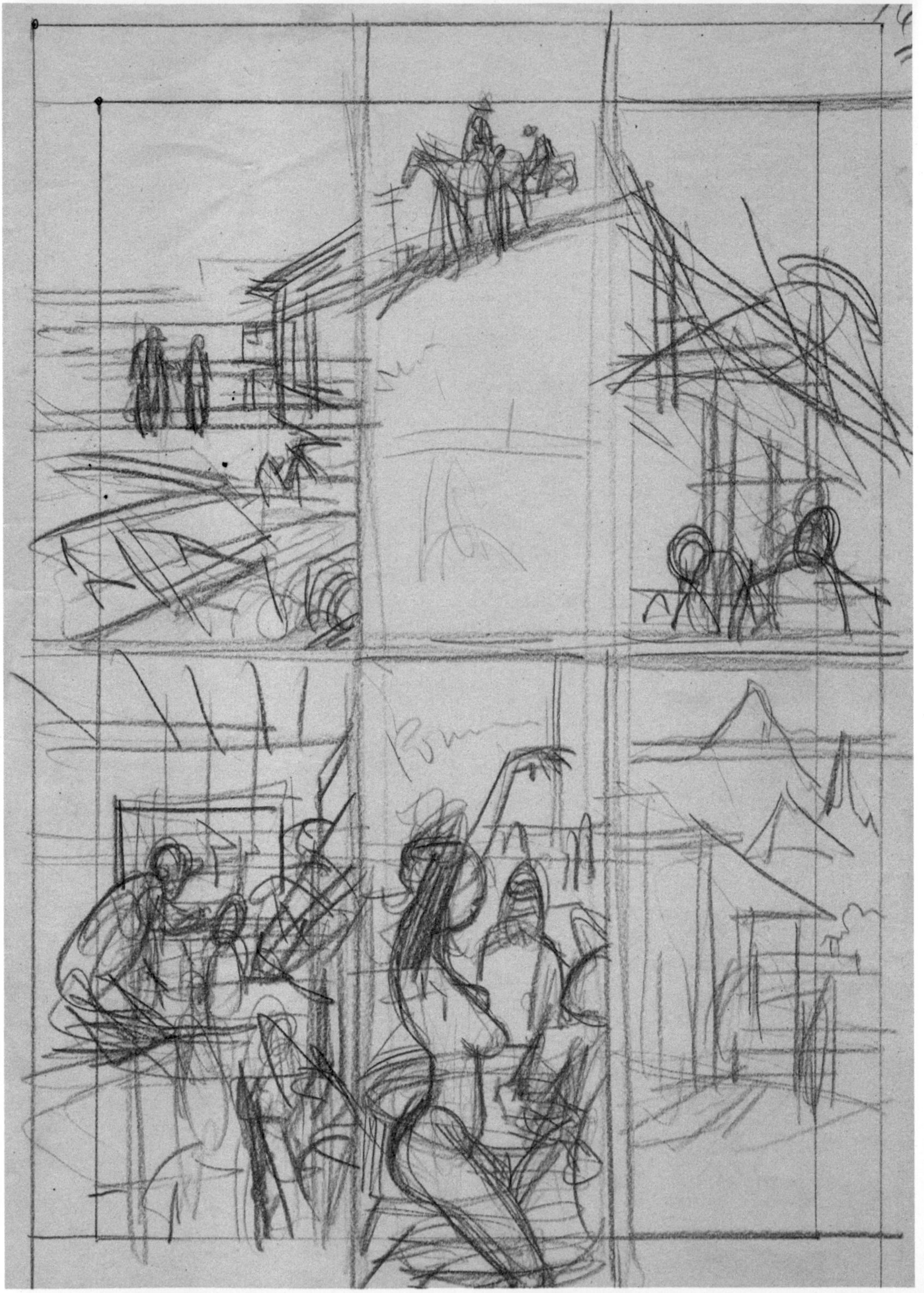

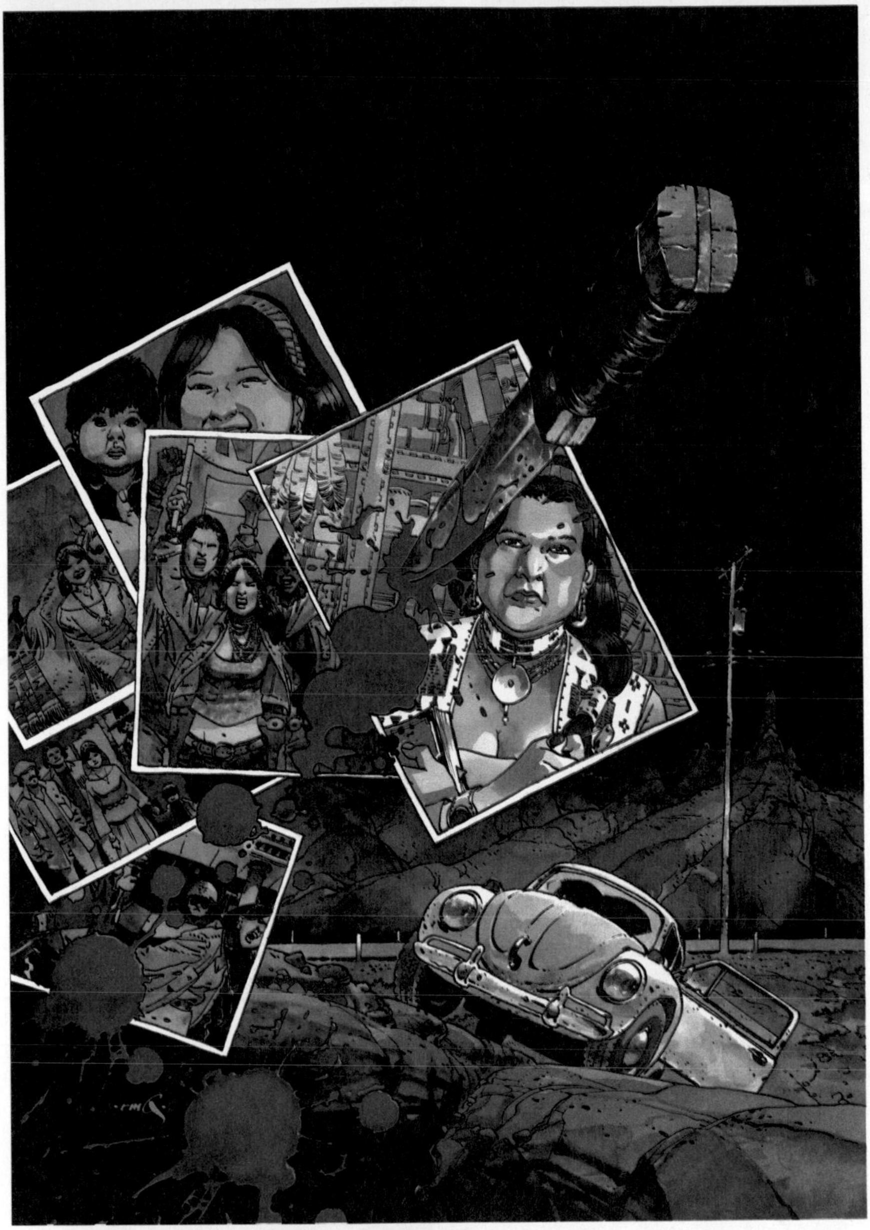

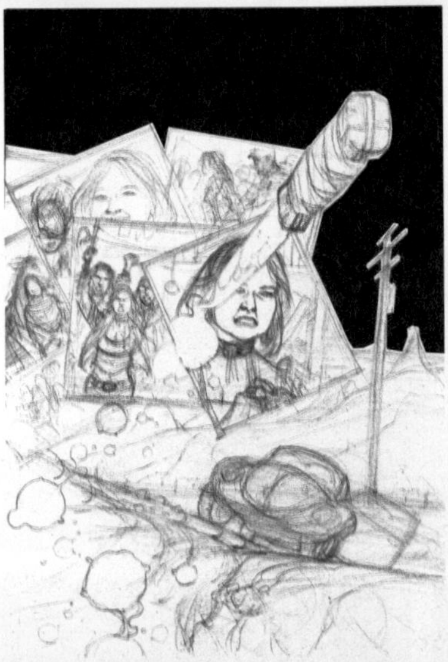

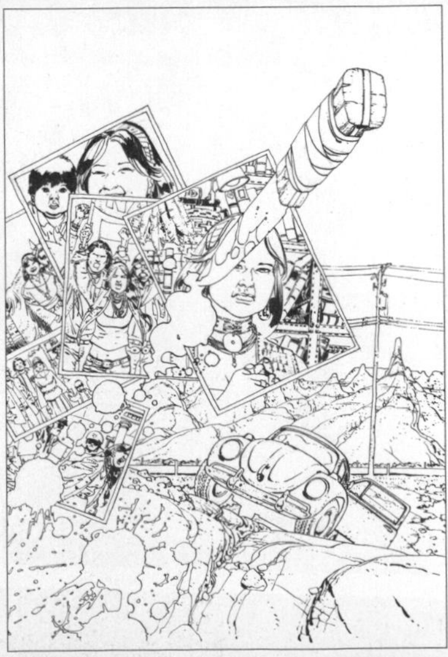

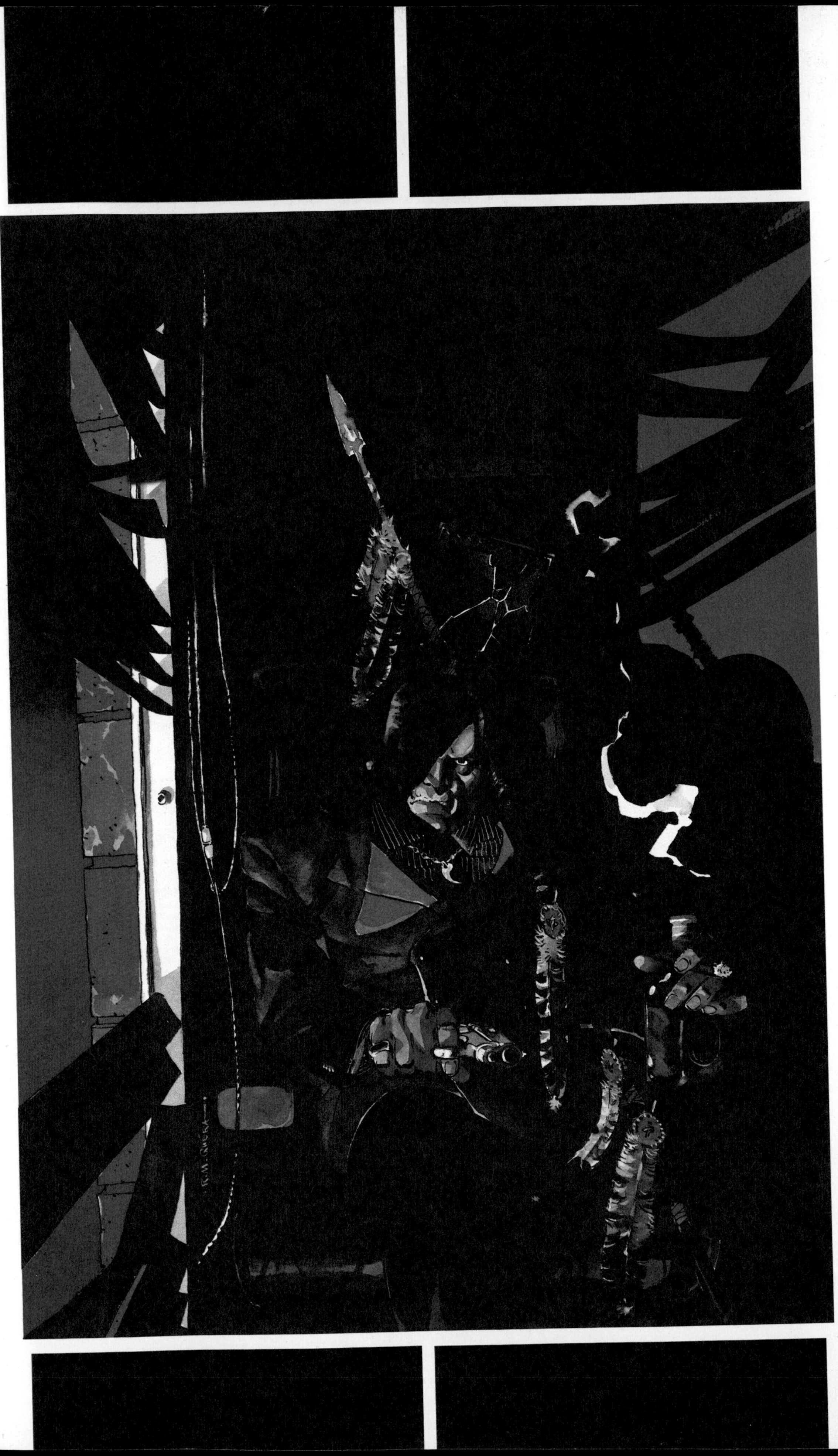
R.M. GUERA

The Prairie Rose Indian Reservation is a third-world nation in the heart of America, in South Dakota, under the very shadow of Mt. Rushmore. More than half of its residents live below the federal poverty level. Eighty percent are unemployed. The infant mortality rate is the highest on this continent. Adolescent suicide is four times the national average. Alcoholism affects eight out of ten families. Even though alcohol is illegal on the reservation, sales at liquor stores along the border with Nebraska average $3.5 million a year. Most homes on the reservation are substandard, with no electricity, telephone or running water. All told, the residents of Prairie Rose have the shortest life expectancy in the entire Western Hemisphere.

Yet despite all that, these people endure.

These are the Lakota, the Ikche-Wichasha, as they call themselves ("the Real Natural Human Beings"). These are the people of Sitting Bull and Crazy Horse. The warriors who annihilated Custer's 7th Cavalry at the Battle of Little Bighorn. The last major Indian tribe to put down their rifles and make peace with the U.S. government.

For 120 years, these Lakota have been confined to a rugged stretch of hardscrabble land in the Badlands of South Dakota, forced to endure religious boarding schools where they were beaten for speaking their native language, forced sterilization at the hands of the Indian Health Service and government polices that have run the gamut from eradication to assimilation to neglect.

In the 1970s, many Lakota again took up arms and demanded their rights, and this militant "Red Power" movement quickly came into conflict with the FBI, turning the reservation into a war zone. For a while, this reservation of 20,000 people had the highest murder rate in the United States.

Now the Lakota face a new challenge, one that will either lift them at last from poverty or plunge them deeper into despair. A new casino is being built on the rez, and with it comes internal strife. On one side, you have the traditionalists who fear the crime and corruption that a casino will bring, believing instead that only a return to the Old Ways can help the Lakota to thrive once again. On the other side, you have the progressives, who welcome the casino and what they see as a chance to finally start taking reparations from the white man, one bloody nickel at a time if they have to.

This is the world of SCALPED. A world of shotgun-shack meth labs and million-dollar casinos. Of high-stakes poker games and trailer park dog fights. A world of brutality and deep-seated spirituality. Of double-crosses, broken treaties and undercover feds.

JASON AARON

Jason Aaron is an Eisner and Harvey award-nominated comic
book writer whose best-known work includes the Native
American crime drama SCALPED for DC's Vertigo imprint
and the acclaimed *Southern Bastards* (co-created with artist
Jason Latour) for Image. He also wrote several well-regarded
runs on a number of titles for Marvel Comics, including
Wolverine, *Ghost Rider* and *Thor.* Aaron was born in
Alabama and currently resides in Kansas City. He enjoys many things,
but shaving is not one of them.

R.M. GUÉRA

Born in Yugoslavia, comic book artist R.M. Guéra has lived in Spain since 1991. His
internationally published work includes two volumes of the French series *Le Lièvre de Mars*,
written by Patrick Cothias and published by Glénat, and the critically acclaimed Native
American crime series SCALPED, written by Jason Aaron and published by Vertigo. He
has also illustrated BATMAN ETERNAL for DC Comics, as well as the comics adaptation of
Quentin Tarantino's DJANGO UNCHAINED for Vertigo.

DAVIDE FURNÒ

Davide Furnò is an Italian artist known in the U.S. for his work on the Vertigo series SCALPED
and GREEK STREET, as well as IDW's *30 Days of Night*, *24* and *Infestation*. In Italy, Furnò's art
has appeared in such series as *Dylan Dog* and *Saguaro* for publisher Sergio Bonelli Editore
and on the covers of a line of *noir* titles for publisher Edizioni BD. Furnò also teaches at the
International School of Comics in Rome, and he recently illustrated the Caped Crusader for
an issue of BATMAN: ETERNAL.

JOHN PAUL LEON

An alumnus of New York City's School of Visual Arts, John Paul Leon has been working in
comics for more than 25 years. Some of his notable credits include the critically acclaimed
series *Earth X*, THE WINTER MEN, STATIC and MOTHER PANIC. He has also provided covers
for such titles as DETECTIVE COMICS, DMZ, *The Massive* and SAVAGE THINGS. Leon lives
in Miami, Florida and is currently working on BATMAN: CREATURE OF THE NIGHT for DC
Comics.